The Name

OTHER BOOKS BY FRANKLIN GRAHAM

Rebel with a Cause
Miracle in a Shoebox
Living Beyond the Limits

The Name

Franklin
GRAHAM

WITH

BRUCE NYGREN

NELSON BOOKS
A Division of Thomas Nelson Publishers
Since 1798

www.thomasnelson.com

Published in Nashville, Tennessee, by Thomas Nelson, Inc.

Library of Congress Cataloging-in-Publication Data

Graham, Franklin, 1952–
The name / Franklin Graham
p. cm.
ISBN 0-7852-6522-8 (hc)
ISBN 0-7852-6080-3 (sc)
ISBN 0-7852-6361-6 (ie)
1. Jesus Christ—Name. 2. Names in the Bible. I. Title.
BT590.N2 G73 2002
232—dc 2002008318

Printed in the United States of America

04 05 06 07 08 PHX 5 4 3 2 1

To the late Dr. Roy W. Gustafson,
a longtime friend and associate
and a man who made a profound impact on my life.
He was a great counselor and friend.

CONTENTS

The Name

1

BLASTING THE NAME

"Christianity is a religion for losers," said one famous American billionaire.[1]

"Organized religion is a sham and a crutch for weak-minded people who need strength in numbers," said a famous American politician.[2]

It makes no sense! What drives two such otherwise intelligent, motivated, and successful men to publicly slam the followers of the greatest Name in history?

The wealthy man founded a television network, owns two sports teams, and several ranches in the United States. He is an outstanding yachtsman who once won sailing's prestigious America's Cup. *Time* magazine once selected him "Man of the Year," and he is generous in supporting favorite charities and causes. Even though he may apologize later, this man has a habit of bashing Christians. Why does a brilliant man like Ted Turner go out of his way to blast believers loyal to the Name?

Then there's the politician. As a young man, he valiantly served his country as a Navy SEAL. Later he made a name for himself as a professional wrestler and actor. He has served as a volunteer for organizations like the Make a Wish Foundation. His entry into politics was as the mayor of a large suburb adjoining a major American city. In 1998, he shocked the political world with his election as a third-party candidate to the governor's chair. With so many outstanding credits to his name, why does Governor Jesse Ventura of the great state of Minnesota say that religion is just for the "weak-minded"?

In recent times it has almost become a requirement for the sophisticated and intelligent to take a swipe at the nearest Christian. A recent magazine article explained how to many of the "culturally elite," the enemy of civilization is not terrorism but instead religious believers of "all types, including orthodox Jews and Christians."[3]

Some years ago, I remember hearing how the then secretary-general of the United Nations, U Thant, spoke openly of his beliefs. On one occasion he said, "I ever believe that the mark of a truly educated and imaginative person facing the twenty-first century is that he feels himself to be a planetary being. Perhaps my own Buddhist upbringing has helped me more than anything else to realize and to express in my speeches and writings this concept of world citizenship. As a Buddhist I was trained to be tolerant of everything except intolerance."[4] A friend told me that he once heard U Thant say publicly that all he had he owed to Buddha.

I have no problem with allowing any person to express his or her views on their personal faith—this being one of the freedoms we enjoy in America. Can you imagine, though, the outrage that would occur today if someone in a similar position spoke as candidly about personal Christian faith?

Maybe we should not be so shocked; people have been taking potshots at Jesus for more than twenty centuries. Even one who was to become an ardent disciple started out as a skeptic. When Nathaniel first heard about the remarkable young Carpenter from down the road, his response was, "Can anything good come out of Nazareth?"[5] Later Jesus' own family members expressed doubt. Jesus told them that the world "hates Me because I testify . . . that its works are evil."[6] On another occasion, Jesus explained that those who follow Him would face trials and persecution. He was right. As the centuries have rolled by, the Name and its followers have encountered opposition. The nineteenth-century atheist philosopher Friedrich Nietzsche said, "Jesus died too soon. He would have repudiated His doctrine if He had lived to my age."[7] Nietzsche was so hostile that he wrote a book entitled *The Antichrist* in which he said:

> I condemn Christianity; I bring against the Christian Church the most terrible of all the accusations that an accuser has ever had in his mouth . . . The Christian Church has left nothing untouched by its depravity; it has turned every value into worthlessness, and every truth into a lie, and every integrity into baseness of soul.[8]

Others have been more or less acidic, but still critical. Mark Twain, with typical biting wit, said: "If Christ were here now there is one thing he would not be—a Christian."[9]

In the twentieth century, the twin evils of Nazism and Communism produced some of the Name's most venomous foes. Adolf Hitler, who was a "philosophic disciple" of his fellow German Nietzsche, had some demented words of his own to describe Christians:

> We are fighting against the most ancient curse that humanity has brought upon itself. We are fighting against the perversion of our soundest instincts. Ah, the God of the deserts, that crazed, stupid, vengeful Asiatic despot with his powers to make laws! That poison with which both Jews and Christians have spoiled and soiled the free, wonderful instincts of man and lowered them to the level of doglike fright.[10]

Hitler, along with Lenin, Stalin, and Mao, denounced Christianity in advancing his demonic schemes and atheistic Communist propaganda.

Even entertainers join the bashing. John Lennon of the Beatles made big waves when he said, "Christianity will go. It will vanish and shrink. I needn't argue with that; I'm right and I will be proved right. We're more popular than Jesus now: I don't know which will go first—rock and roll or Christianity."[11]

Today, the Beatles have dispersed. Members of the band have stepped through the portals of eternity to stand before God in heaven. Overwhelmingly, though, the Name of Jesus and what He taught and did—and insisted His followers do—continue to transform lives.

The Apostle Peter reminds all believers: "If you are insulted because of the name of Christ, you are blessed, for the Spirit of glory and of God rests on you . . . If you suffer as a Christian, do not be ashamed, but praise God that you bear that name."[12]

Historian Philip Schaff described the overwhelming influence that Jesus had on subsequent history and culture of the world:

> This Jesus of Nazareth, without money and arms, conquered more millions than Alexander, Caesar, Mohammed, and Napoleon; without science . . . he shed more light on things human and divine than all philosophers and scholars combined; without the eloquence of schools, he spoke such words of life as were never spoken before or since, and produced effects which lie beyond the reach of orator or poet; without writing a single line, he set more pens in motion, and furnished themes for more sermons, orations, discussions, learned volumes, works of art, and songs of praise than the whole army of great men of ancient and modern times.[13]

One of the great military geniuses of all time, Napoleon I, wrote:

> I know men; and I tell you that Jesus Christ is not a man. Superficial minds see a resemblance between Christ and the founders of empires, and the gods of other religions. That resemblance does not exist. There is between Christianity and whatever other religions the distance of infinity . . . Everything in Christ astonishes me . . . I search in vain in history to find the similar to Jesus Christ, or anything which can approach the Gospel. Neither history, nor humanity, nor the ages, nor nature, offer me anything with which I am able to compare it or to explain it.[14]

Author H. G. Wells said, "Christ is the most unique person in history. No man can write a history of the human race without giving first and foremost place to the penniless teacher of Nazareth."[15]

Wolfgang Amadeus Mozart, one of the greatest composers and pianists in all of history, said:

> It is a great consolation for me to remember that the Lord, to whom I had drawn near in humble and child-like faith, has suffered and died for me, and that He will look on me in love and compassion.

Alexis de Tocqueville, the French statesman, historian, and philosopher, observed:

> In the United States the sovereign authority is religious, . . . there is no country in the world where the Christian religion retains a greater influence over the souls of men than in America, and there can be no greater proof of its utility and of its conformity to human nature than that its influence is powerfully felt over the most enlightened and free nation of the earth.

President Theodore Roosevelt, one of the great populist presidents who with his swashbuckling style charged San Juan Hill, explored Africa, and took the American flag across the globe, said:

> After a week on perplexing problems it does so rest my soul to . . . come into the house of The Lord and to sing and mean it, "Holy, Holy, Holy, Lord God Almighty" . . . [my] great joy and glory that, in occupying an exalted position in the nation, I am enabled, to preach the practical moralities of The Bible to my fellow-countrymen and to hold up Christ as the hope and Savior of the world.

After all these centuries, just why is the Name so controversial and still stirring such a brew of conflicting passions?

Answering that question is the single task of this book. It is important for you to know much about the Name. This is not just another interesting spiritual topic. An understanding of the Name is the key to all of life. The Apostle Paul hit the nail on the head concerning the Lord Jesus Christ when he wrote the following to the Christians at Colosse:

> He is the image of the invisible God, the firstborn over all creation. For by him all things were created: things in heaven and on earth, visible and invisible, whether thrones or powers or rulers or authorities; all things were created by him and for him. He is before all things, and in him all things hold together. And he is the head of the body, the church; he is the beginning and the firstborn from among the dead, so that in everything he might have the supremacy. For God was pleased to have all his fullness dwell in him, and through him to reconcile to himself all things, whether things on earth or things in heaven, by making peace through his blood, shed on the cross.[16]

The Ted Turners, Jesse Venturas, and others who ridicule or demean the Name and His followers must not understand what they are doing and whom they are dealing with. Unfortunately, the fence-sitters and even many who follow the Lord Jesus do not grasp the incredible scope and impact of His life either.

That is why I have written *The Name*.

The Name stands before, beyond, and after all others.

In the beginning was the Name. At the end will be the Name. In the present time, all things depend upon the Name.

The Name is above all names.

The Name will cause all knees to bow . . . Jesse's, Ted's, yours, mine . . . for all time.

Do you know the Name?

Are you allied with the Name?

Your life or death depends upon your answers.

* * *

How can any name be that important?

Most of us do not think too much about names—ours or anyone else's.

That certainly was my attitude toward my name for a long time. My family name arrived on American soil long ago by way of my Scottish ancestors—the Grahams actually settled in the Carolinas before the American Revolution.

Growing up, I did not understand or appreciate my family name. Since I was the son of a well-known preacher, people assumed either the worst or the best about me. The "worst" was that I was a pampered, spoiled brat. The "best," that I was some sort of angelic being living by high standards no one could ever achieve. To be honest, I have never been an angel. If you asked my sisters, they would likely tell you what I really was growing up—a terror.

Later in life, I became more aware that being a Graham and the son of a famous man might have an upside and a downside. The upside was that I was able to meet some interesting people and go to some interesting places. When I was thirteen, President Lyndon Johnson invited my father to spend the night at the White House. Daddy took me along, and guess what? I slept in the Lincoln Bedroom! Since then, I have had the privilege of meeting every U.S. president.

The downside of bearing my family name was people's unrealistic expectations. It was not until I was in my twenties, after fully committing my life to the Lord, that I took much more seriously the privilege and responsibility I had because of my father. I knew that if I did something disgraceful, it would not just embarrass me but bring shame to my family's name that so many people in the world admired.

When I began my ministry at Samaritan's Purse I traveled around the world visiting the ministry's relief efforts. Everywhere I went, people approached me and expressed delight that I was the son of Billy Graham. Often they were shy and apologetic, thinking that what they had to say was of little interest because I had heard similar stories many times before. They just had to tell me how my father's ministry had impacted their own spiritual journeys: "We know you must get tired of hearing this, but I wanted you to know . . . And if you ever think of it, when you are with your father, would you please tell him 'thank you'?"

Truthfully, I never tire of hearing how individuals or their relatives or friends came to know peace with God through the life and ministry of Billy Graham. I rejoice. Often after their life-changing encounter with Jesus Christ, these people went on to do great things themselves, touching thousands of others in His Name.

I know now that the times I missed my father when he was away for extended periods were all worth it—every minute. I do not want to hurt the name of my earthly father, or the Name of my Father in heaven.

However, there are times when linkage to a well-known name is challenging. Words spoken in private may become tomorrow's headlines and may be completely misunderstood or misquoted. That can make one's life certainly more challenging. However, those challenges often lead to unprecedented opportunities to serve the Lord. For me, I want to be faithful in bearing the Name of the Lord Jesus Christ.

ROAMING THE DESERT

One of the great challenges in my ministry has been the work we do in difficult places. Over the years, I have worked extensively throughout Lebanon, Egypt, Jordan, Syria, and even Iraq. This is an area of the world that I love.

In some areas of the Middle East today, life has not changed much from Bible times. I have personally seen people living in goat-hair tents. I have witnessed camel caravans traveling across the desert. Seeing this makes the Bible come alive, especially as I read about Abraham, who searched for the land that God promised. I have a great love for the Arab people and have many personal friends who have given their lives to serve them.

One of my longtime friends, Aileen Coleman, is a missionary nurse who has served the Arab people for decades in the Middle East with modern medical care all in the Name of Jesus Christ. Our ministry, Samaritan's Purse, has assisted her on a number of occasions. Aileen told me a true story concerning the Bedouin tribes who still roam that land today.

"Bedouin" is an Aramaic name for desert dwellers. These people, perhaps strange to us, are rich in tradition and custom, much of which is very closely aligned to biblical teachings. These nomads are descendants of Abraham and Sarah's Egyptian handmaid, Hagar, and are often to be found speaking about "our great father, Abraham." He, too, lived in goat-hair tents, as did Isaac and Jacob, and they would be very much at home today among these wanderers of the desert. This story took place in the southern part of the Hashemite Kingdom of Jordan near Wadi Rum, a bleak and barren desert area well-known to the Bedouin people.

The story illustrates so powerfully in human terms the many facets of strength, protection, love, redemption, and power found through the integrity a name holds.

SAFE IN A TENT

As two boys, Abdul and Mohammed, were climbing the rocky terrain one day, they wound up in a heated argument. Abdul struck and accidentally killed Mohammed. As with others of different races and cultures, the Middle Eastern temper has a very low boiling point. Most of the time they vent their volatile emotions with ear-splitting cursing, flailing of their arms, and often with the flashing of gold-capped teeth. This young man had lost control, and now his friend lay dead on the stony landscape, a victim of second-degree murder. Abdul experienced the ultimate horror. Looking down, Abdul's heart sickened as he saw the limp body of his friend.

"Mohammed!" Abdul screamed.

Mohammed lay strangely still, his neck twisted.

"Mohammed, Mohammed!" Abdul shrieked, but Mohammed did not answer. Abdul shook him, trying desperately to get a response from his best friend. The lifeless body lay twisted on the jagged rocks. Abdul began to sob, the tears stinging his weather-beaten cheeks.

Mohammed was dead.

In Bedouin society, "an eye for an eye, life for a life" still prevails. Knowing the inflexible custom of his people, this young man ran across the desert in terror until he spotted the sprawling tent of the tribal chief. The youth, gasping for air, raced to the shelter, grabbed hold of the tent peg, and screamed for mercy. When the sheik heard the boy's cry he came to the door. The young man confessed his guilt and asked for protection.

It is a Bedouin custom that if a fugitive grabs hold of a tent peg and pleads for protection from the owner of that tent, if the owner grants protection, he will lay down his life for the one on the run. It is a matter of honor and duty; the integrity of the owner's name is on the line.

The sheik looked at the frantic young man, his knuckles white from gripping the tent peg so tightly. The old sheik put his hand on one of the guy-ropes of his tent and swore by Allah. "Go inside," the sheik said to the boy with a wave. "I give you my protection."

The next day, young men who had witnessed the crime came running toward the tent, shouting, "There he is! There's the killer!"

But the old man said, "I have given my word."

Now the boy's life depended on this old Bedouin's integrity.

"Out of the way! Give us the boy!" they yelled.

The old Bedouin sheik stood his ground. His name was respected in the village. His word was good. If these men, intent on revenge, laid a hand on Abdul, they would have to kill the old man first.

"Stand aside, sheik," a man yelled. "Give us the boy!"

The old man stood strong. "No." His voice rang out as he slipped his hand around the knife hanging around his waist.

"You don't understand," the pursuers argued. "That boy is a murderer. He has taken the life of another."

"I've promised him my protection. I will honor my oath," the sheik replied.

"Do you know who he killed?" the men argued.

"It doesn't matter," the sheik replied.

One of the men blurted out, "He killed your son—your only son!"

The old man flinched as if a knife had pierced his heart. His eyes filled with tears. There was a long silence. The old man's knees weakened. His face tensed.

On the floor of the sheik's tent, Abdul closed his eyes and buried his face, awaiting retaliation. Surely this was the end.

After a few moments, the old man softly spoke, "I'm an old man; I'll never be able to have another son."

Abdul felt his heart race. *I'm dead,* he thought.

"I have given the boy my protection," the sheik continued, "and I will honor my oath."

"What?" The pursuers were stunned. "How can you honor your oath when he's the one responsible for your son's death?"

In a hushed voice the sheik said again, "I am an old man. I cannot bring my son back to life. Because this boy came to me in the right way, I will take him as my own son and raise him. He will live in my tent and will be my heir. All that I have will be his. He will bear my name."

* * *

When I heard Aileen tell this story chills rushed through me. This was a picture of what God has done for mankind through the death of the One who bears the Name.

Just as with Abdul, eternal life or death for each of us depends on our finding protection, refuge, and redemption through the shed blood of Jesus Christ. As the Bible says, "Whoever calls on the name of the LORD shall be saved."[17]

The Apostle John said, "But as many as received Him, to them He gave the right to become children of God, to those who believe in His name."[18]

Believing in the Name of God's only Son is the real issue. From John's statement two thousand years ago until today, a conflict has raged over this Name. The greatest controversy in history was, and still is, this Name. Why has this Name shaken the very foundations of human society? As you read the chapters ahead, you decide.

2

"YOU OFFENDED ME"

It was a cloudy, gray Sunday afternoon in Colorado. The weather matched the mood. Several dozen of us—most wearing shades of black along with a small silver-and-blue ribbon—sat quietly with our thoughts, waiting for the memorial service to begin.

We were seated outdoors, on a makeshift stage that usually served as the entrance to a multiplex theater. Bouquets of flowers scented the cold mountain air. A temporary roof, draped with banners, provided some protection from an intermittent mist. In the distance, light snow whitened the front range of the Rocky Mountains.

An estimated crowd of seventy thousand had gathered in the expansive parking lot before us. The spring air chilled the mourners, who clutched blue and white balloons. Many held flowers. Some hoisted homemade signs expressing their feelings of loss and grief.

I love Colorado and have since 1974 when my wife, Jane, and I as newlyweds drove a jeep from North Carolina to Estes Park to attend a small Bible school. I always look forward to visiting this beautiful state. However, on this particularly dreary day, I wished I could have been anywhere other than this Rocky Mountain city. What would I say? What *could* I say?

The tragedy on the prior Tuesday, April 20, 1999, had interrupted television network soap operas and talk shows with an alarming news bulletin: A high school in suburban Denver was under siege. Details were sparse, but first reports indicated that gunmen were on a killing spree inside the school. Hundreds of police, firefighters, and SWAT personnel wearing protective gear and bearing weapons had arrived. As helicopters hovered overhead, the officers crouched behind squad cars and peered around walls. A convoy of ambulances with sirens wailing appeared. What was happening on this spring morning in one of America's more pristine and affluent communities?

Like most Americans, I had never heard of Columbine High School, yet millions of us stopped what we were doing to watch the shocking images on the television screen: terrified students running for their lives; a boy hanging out a window, then falling into the arms of rescuers; tearful reunions of children and parents.

We watched and prayed. Before long, the story began to unfold. Two teenage boys, filled with hate and driven by evil, had spewed their venom with bullets and bombs on innocent students and staff. The carnage stopped only when Eric Harris and Dylan Klebold turned their guns on themselves in the school's library. They had murdered twelve students and one teacher.

The day following the massacre, on April 21, the CNN producer for *Larry King Live* called. Larry planned to devote that evening's television program to the Columbine massacre and invited me to comment on this unspeakable tragedy. I agreed, and later drove to a nearby studio where I could join Larry's program via a remote "feed." Before going on the air, I was able, by TV monitor, to watch Larry's interview with another guest, a teenage girl by the name of Mickie Cain, a student who had witnessed much of the preceding day's events. She was having a difficult time maintaining her composure and was able to blurt out only a few words before lapsing into uncontrollable sobs.

Larry was patient and gave the young girl plenty of time to regain her composure. She recounted the chilling story: "Let me tell you about my friend Cassie. She was amazing. She ended up standing for the greatest thing ever. She had the courage to turn her life around and started trusting Christ. She completely stood up for God when the killers asked her if there was anyone [in the classroom] who had faith in Christ. She spoke up and they shot her for it."

I was stunned. I could not believe what I had just heard. If this story was true, then a Christian martyr's blood had stained the carpet of an American high school.

As I watched I could not help but think back to my ancestors in Scotland who, when ordered to recognize the King of England as the head of the church, refused, proclaiming, "The Lord Jesus Christ is the only true head of the church." Thousands who professed this were massacred because they would not turn their backs on the Name of the Lord Jesus Christ. Scots came by the boatload to the shores of America. Why? So that they could worship the Lord Jesus Christ with freedom from fear and death.

As I was contemplating all of this, Larry King brought me on the air, giving me an opportunity to comment on what Mickie Cain had declared to the world about her friend. As a Christian I knew that Cassie Bernall was now safe in her heavenly Father's care. She had declared her loyalty to Christ and died for His Name.

Two days later, an aide to Governor Owens of Colorado called. A memorial service had been scheduled for Sunday afternoon. The governor asked me to join government officials and others in honoring the slain and to bring a short message of hope. With fear and hesitation, I accepted the invitation.

I flew to Denver and stayed with close friends Bill and Verna Pauls. The memorial service was not until the next day, but I wanted to go that afternoon to an impromptu memorial site that attracted thousands of mourners. We drove as near to the school as we could get. People drifted between the school, roped off as a crime scene, and a nearby city park that had become a memorial site. Flowers, balloons, cards, stuffed animals, and other mementos of remembrance were stacked high. Walking near, I saw a huge mound of flowers and learned that the car of one of the victims, Rachel Scott, was entombed under that unstructured bouquet. A reverent silence permeated the whole area. Mourners stood in groups, whispering to one another, like awestruck visitors seeing a majestic cathedral for the first time. Thousands of notes and cards were placed on the ground. One note in a child's handwriting said, "Dear God, teach me how to laugh again."

Now, a day later, along with many dignitaries, we waited quietly for the memorial service to begin. Vice President Al Gore and his wife, Tipper, arrived with Governor Owens, the mayor, as well as school and city officials. The service began as two brothers, students at the high school, sang a song of tribute they had written called "Friend of Mine." The lyrics said,

> Can you still hear raging guns, ending dreams of precious ones?
> In God's Son, hope will come; His red stain will take our pain.

During the song, someone in the crowd released a balloon into the air. Another followed. Then dozens. Hundreds. Finally—as if on cue—thousands of the blue and white balloons filled the sky. It was one of many intensely moving moments. All of us, including the vice president, fixed our eyes toward heaven as this vast array of balloons faded from sight.

Next, a band of kilt-wearing bagpipers played "Amazing Grace." I saw hundreds of tearstained faces. The crowd filled the parking lot and seemed to stretch out of sight. In the distance, perched like giant birds, several people watched from the limbs of a leafless tree.

One after another, dignitaries and guests offered healing words and prayers. Amy Grant, Phil Driscoll, and my good friend Michael W. Smith comforted the audience with music. Michael sang his popular song "Friends," and as the music rang through the P.A. system, students and adults swayed arm in arm. After Retired General Colin Powell was introduced, Vice President Gore spoke with compassion: "Here in Jefferson County, the spring has yielded a cold winter of the heart." As he spoke, I prayed silently, *Lord, when I speak, help me lift up the Name of Your Son.*

I had struggled to prepare. What do you say to the heartbroken at such a painful time? I have learned from years of disaster relief work, viewing the aftermath of wars, natural disasters and human cruelty of every kind, that there is only one message that brings comfort and hope. More accurately, there is only one Person who brings comfort and hope in times like these. As I stood to speak, I saw the faces of the thirteen families seated that had lost loved ones.

I spoke about Job in the Bible; how he had asked God "Why?" after he had suffered loss. Like you, I have often heard people ask, "Why?" We all have asked the same thing. I told the crowd that I had no answer to that question but I was sure of this: "There is a God. He loves you. He cares for you. One day He will judge all men. One day He will bring justice. One day, my friends, He will make all things right."

With conviction I said, "God understands loss—the loss of this world to sin. The loss of His Son, the Lord Jesus Christ, as He hung on Calvary's cross, as He gave His life for our sins.

"Jesus understands loss. When Jesus heard of the death of His good friend Lazarus, He wept. He knows your pain. He sees your tears, and He offers what He offered to Lazarus—resurrection to a new life. Eternal life with Him: Jesus said, 'I am the resurrection and the life. He who believes in Me, though he may die, he shall live. And whoever lives and believes in Me shall never die.'"[1]

Then I asked those listening, "Do you believe in the Lord Jesus?" and I shared the Good News of the Gospel. The mist from banks of low clouds had become a drizzle. The crowd was nearly covered by a canopy of multicolored umbrellas. On such a gray, sad afternoon, all I could do as a minister of the Gospel was to speak of the only Light that can pierce life's darkest hours.

I reminded the crowd of the life-or-death decision made by Cassie Bernall. "As the killer rushed into the library and pointed his gun and asked her the life-or-death question, 'Do you believe in God?' she paused and then answered, 'Yes. I believe.' Those were the last words this brave, seventeen-year-old Christian would ever say. The gunman took her earthly life. I believe that Cassie immediately went into the presence of Almighty God. She was ready."

Applause honoring Cassie's sacrifice rose from the crowd.

"She was ready to meet God and to stand before Him," I continued. "My question to you today is, 'Are you ready?' Life is full of change. To be prepared we must be willing to confess our sins, repent of our sins, and ask God for His forgiveness, and to receive His Son, Jesus Christ, by faith into our hearts and into our lives. God will forgive us, and He will cleanse us of all our sin. He will give us a new heart, a new spirit, and a new beginning. And He will give us the hope and the assurance that one day we will be with Him in heaven."

Again, I urged everyone there to put their faith and hope in the Lord Jesus Christ and, after praying, sat down.

Governor Owens thanked me and closed the service. As he read the names of the victims, a white dove was set free to fly in remembrance of each one slain. "God grant them eternal peace," the governor said.

Four military jets streaked through the sky and a rabbi, from the Denver area, closed the service with a prayer. The bagpipers and drum corps led the platform party as we walked to the Columbine memorial site where flowers were placed as a final act honoring the dead.

As the march began, a man approached me. He was obviously agitated and said in a loud, obnoxious voice, "You offended me!"

I was stunned. I did not even know this man. How had I offended him? Not wanting to engage in an argument—especially at a time like this—I looked him directly in the eye and with a soft voice replied, "Yes, sir?"

Bewildered by my reply, he said again, "You offended me!" and I replied again, "Yes, sir?" He acted as though I should know what he was talking about, but I was puzzled. To argue would have been disgraceful at such a solemn moment.

The man said again, "You offended me!" and I said again, "Yes, sir." Then he walked away. I began to review what I had said from the platform. Had my use of the Name of Jesus caused offense?

My hunch was right. In the following days, the local newspapers reported the story of my so-called "offense" at the Columbine memorial service. Another man, the president of a liberal interfaith organization, was quoted in the *Denver Post:* "I felt like he [Franklin Graham] was trying to terrorize us into heaven instead of loving us into heaven."[2]

Others said they were offended because I used the Name of Jesus. However, I also received many letters and calls from people who were thankful for what I had said and expressed their support.

Misty Bernall, Cassie's mother, called the week after the Columbine service and thanked me for presenting the truth of the Gospel. We talked about God's truth being the only source of hope. Mrs. Bernall shared with me a little about Cassie's life. A few years before the Columbine school tragedy, Cassie had strayed from the Lord. Her parents felt that they were losing Cassie to Satan's grip. They grounded her from all activity except going to church. One weekend while on a youth retreat, Cassie came face-to-face with the truth of God's Word. In a real sense, Cassie came to know Him, and the truth of His love had set her free from sin's bondage.

From the Columbine tragedy came a renewed focus concerning the impact of the Name. Just why is it that the Name of the Lord Jesus causes such a fuss? Why is it that when people curse using His Name, hardly anyone complains; but if you speak about Him with respect or pray in His Name, some people cry "foul," like the man who said, "You offended me." Let's explore what it is about the Name that brings such comfort and healing to millions as it has throughout the ages . . . yet provokes in others such venomous hatred and offense.

3

PRAY IN THE NAME?

There are factions of society today that hate God and everything that He stands for. But I did not expect such a vehement backlash. In America, where our currency declares "In God We Trust," it still surprises me that when a Christian minister does what he is ordained to do—read and quote from the Bible, share the truth of the Gospel, pray in the Name of Jesus—some people view those acts as borderline subversive!

In January of 2001, our nation was perhaps more divided politically than at any time I can remember. The controversy surrounding the presidential election vote count in Florida had polarized Americans. Even though most voters were pleased to see a change in the White House after eight turbulent years, according to pollsters, nearly 50 percent were disappointed and even convinced that Governor Bush and the Republicans had somehow manipulated the outcome. In hindsight, election officials and even the media concurred, after intense scrutiny and review, that this was not the case.

My father has had the honor of praying or participating in some way at eight presidential inaugurations, beginning with the ceremony for Lyndon Johnson in 1965. When it came time for Bill Clinton's second inauguration, my father was invited once again to offer an inaugural prayer. Because his health problems had flared, he asked me to accompany him to Washington, D.C.

During that ceremony, I was seated at my father's right side on the inaugural platform. To my left sat all of the Supreme Court justices in their robes and caps. Behind was the Democratic and Republican leadership from both houses of Congress.

This spectacular event always involves much pomp and circumstance. The election battle is over. The time now comes for the government of this mighty land and its citizens to inaugurate a president.

I had been impressed to see members of the opposing political parties—in heated battle for the prize of the White House just two months before—now shaking hands and greeting each other warmly. Life for both the nation and individuals would move on. Bill Clinton would continue to govern. Bob Dole would return to private life, make speeches, and enjoy other productive activities outside the Senate chamber. What a great nation and system of government.

When the time had come for my father to pray, the only help needed was a firm hand to help him stand.

Following the ceremony the dignitaries and guests had walked up the steps of the Capitol Building to attend the inaugural luncheon hosted by the Joint Congressional Committee on Inaugural Ceremonies. This gathering has long been a tradition and serves to further make the statement that inauguration day symbolizes our unity as a nation. My father had been asked to offer the prayer of blessing for the food, and so he was seated at the head table. I was seated a short distance away, concerned that he would need some help to the podium when it came time to pray. I approached Vice President Al Gore, seated next to my father, and asked if he would assist my father if needed. He graciously agreed and when my father was introduced, Vice President Gore helped him to his feet to make his way to the microphone.

Though the day had been filled with historical pageantry, I was happy to put it all on the back burner and head for the hills of North Carolina and to my mountain home.

Now, four years later as the inauguration of the forty-third president approached, the inaugural committee eagerly wanted Billy Graham to participate in the ceremony. Perhaps more so than for any other president-elect, my father really wanted to do this for George W. Bush. Some years before, while visiting the Bush family at Kennebunkport, Maine, my father and George W. had had a conversation on issues of faith that had made a dramatic impact on Bush's life, as he describes in his biography, *A Charge to Keep*.[1]

However, with weather forecasters predicting a cold, wet January morning in the Washington, D.C., area, my father's doctors at the Mayo Clinic had urged him not to put himself at risk by attending the inauguration, as it would be held outdoors. The Inaugural Committee, on behalf of President-elect Bush, called and asked me to give the invocation in my father's place. I had already been invited to speak at the president's prayer service at Washington National Cathedral the Sunday following the inauguration, but to deliver the invocation at the swearing in was another matter. Years ago I had told my father that I would stand with him and help him in any way I could, so how could I say no? With a deep sense of responsibility, I accepted the invitation and began to prepare. What an opportunity—to pray for the new president and his administration, as well as stand in for the man I love and respect so much. I also saw this as an awesome responsibility that could not be taken lightly.

Rev. Kirbyjon Caldwell, pastor of the large Windsor Village United Methodist Church in suburban Houston, was scheduled to deliver the benediction. Reverend Caldwell was a friend of the Bush family and had introduced George W. at the Republican National Convention the previous summer.

I labored to construct a prayer that would invoke God's power. Millions would be listening. My deep desire was to focus the nation on Almighty God, ask for His blessing upon the incoming president and outgoing administration, and to bring glory to His Name.

The nation was still licking its election wounds. I pondered the turmoil that the country was still feeling as I wondered how I should close the prayer. Many times Christian pastors praying in public forums just finish their prayers with ". . . in the Name of God." But for me to do so would falsify who I am. I would be disobedient by denying the One I follow. I have always prayed in Jesus' Name. I know of no other ground on which a sinner like me can come before a God who is holy.

Here is another way of looking at it. England's Queen Elizabeth knighted my father in December 2001, but he was unable to travel to the United Kingdom to receive this honor. Instead, the queen authorized the British ambassador to the United States to confer the knighthood upon my father in Washington, D.C., on her behalf. What if the ambassador had acted on his own, without Her Majesty giving him that power? His knighthood would have been meaningless. Similarly, we have no basis or authority to come to God any way except through the Lord Jesus Christ—the Representative God Himself personally sent to us when, through our human striving, we could not reach Him.

Years ago as a young man I sensed that if opportunities came for public ministry they were from God. Now He had opened a door. I had been given a larger platform—the opportunity to help direct the eyes of the nation to God. To honor His Son, wasn't even a question. How could I do anything different than to pray in His Name?

The Friday afternoon before the inauguration, I attended a meeting of the platform participants conducted by the Inaugural Committee. We met at a Washington hotel to review the order of service. It was in that conference room where I met Rev. Kirbyjon Caldwell: tall, handsome, articulate—a powerhouse of a preacher. After introductions, his personal warmth made me feel as though we had been longtime friends. We found a few minutes to talk privately, and Reverend Caldwell said, "Franklin, I want to ask you a question. Are you going to pray in the Name of Jesus?"

"Yes," I answered. "I always do."

"Good!" Kirbyjon said, flashing a great big smile. "I am too."

I chuckled to myself and thought, *I like him; he's got guts for Jesus.*

Inauguration day, Saturday, January 21, the forecast had been accurate. Temperatures were near freezing. A chilling drizzle fell from ground-hugging clouds. My father had made a good decision to stay home.

My wife, Jane, and I arrived at the Capitol Building at 9 A.M. and were taken to a holding room with other platform participants. A couple of hours later we were led to the top of the Capitol steps by a marine, where a spokesman announced our arrival over the P.A. system. I was seated in a chair placed in the same spot my father had occupied four years earlier. I could not help but realize how God had used that experience to prepare me for this day. From the noise in front of the Capitol, I could tell a large crowd was assembled, but seeing faces was impossible due to a large bank of TV cameras in front of the stage that blocked the view.

I was struck again by this smooth transfer of power as dignitaries descended the steps and took their seats. Although the presidential election had been vigorously contested in a way unprecedented in American history, the time had come for America to honor and install a new leader. And in spite of political hostilities, our country has always risen to the occasion with dignity.

When the last guests were seated, the president-elect and his family were announced and escorted to the platform as thunderous applause echoed through the fog. Directly in front of me sat the outgoing team of President Bill Clinton and Vice President Al Gore. Across the aisle sat the incoming team of President-elect George W. Bush and Vice President–elect Dick Cheney.

Anticipation swelled. People of such diverse backgrounds and political persuasions had come together in a moment of unity. The Lord, in His sovereign power, was allowing me the privilege of telling others about Someone more important than anyone on that platform—the One bearing the Name above all other names.

The time of invocation came and I made my way to the podium. Speaking into the bitter January air, I offered this prayer to God Almighty as my breath turned to white puffs:

Blessed are You, O Lord, our God.
Yours, O Lord, is the greatness and the power
And the glory and the majesty and the splendor;
For everything in heaven and earth is Yours.
Yours, O Lord, is the kingdom;
You are exalted as head over all.
Wealth and honor come from You;
You are the ruler of all things.
In Your hands are strength and power to exalt
And give strength to all.

I wanted to make clear at the very outset that as great a nation as America is, we are still dependent totally on the mercy of a holy and great God.

As President Lincoln once said,
We have been the recipients of the choicest bounties of heaven.
We have been preserved these many years in peace and prosperity.
We have grown in numbers, wealth, and power,
As no other nation has ever grown.
But we have forgotten God.
It behooves us, then, to humble ourselves before the Offended Power,
To confess our national sins,
And to pray for clemency and forgiveness.

I thought what Lincoln—one of our greatest presidents—had said was perfect for our present hour, in light of the previous eight years. Although in the same time period our country had experienced abundant prosperity, it was important to remember from where all blessings come—the mercy of our heavenly Father.

O Lord,
As we come together on this historic
And solemn occasion to inaugurate once again
A president and vice president,

Teach us afresh that power, wisdom, and salvation
Come only from Your hand.

We pray, O Lord, for
President-elect George W. Bush
And Vice President–elect Richard B. Cheney,
To whom You have entrusted leadership
Of this nation at this moment in history.

We pray that You will help them bring our country together,
So that we may rise above partisan politics
And seek the larger vision of Your will for our nation.
Use them to bring reconciliation between the races
And healing to political wounds,
That we may truly become "one nation under God."

Our country had never had such a difficult and potentially divisive presidential election. Many citizens were bitter and disillusioned by the process and the outcome. There were more angry demonstrators protesting on the streets of Washington, D.C., than at any inauguration since the Vietnam War. We needed supernatural help to forgive one another, to heal wounds, to move on as a united people.

Give our new president and all who advise him
Calmness in the Face of Storms,
Encouragement in the Face of Frustration, and
Humility in the Face of Success.

Of course none of us could have realized, when I asked the Lord to give George W. Bush "calmness in the face of storms," just how great a storm would howl eight months later on Tuesday morning, September 11.

Give them the wisdom to know, and to do, what is right,
And the courage to say no to all that is contrary to Your statutes and
holy law.

Lord, we pray for their families
And especially their wives,
Laura Bush and Lynne Cheney,
That they may sense Your Presence
And know Your Love.

Today we entrust to You
President and Senator Clinton,
And Vice President and Mrs. Gore.

Lead them as they journey through new doors of opportunity to serve others.

Now, O Lord, we dedicate this
Presidential Inaugural Ceremony to You.
May this be the beginning of a new dawn for America
As we humble ourselves before You
And acknowledge You alone
As our Lord, our Savior, and our Redeemer.

Believing God was directing every word of my prayer, I had carefully chosen the word *Redeemer.* Naturally, I was referring to the One who came to give His life for all who will ever draw breath on this planet. The redemption He purchased with the sacrifice of His own blood is available to anyone who will simply accept it—regardless of creed, nationality, religion, race, reputation, or personal history. I knew stating that there is no other Name by which an individual can be saved would grate on some ears and prick certain hearts. However, as a minister of the Gospel, I was not there to stroke the egos of men. My role was to acknowledge the all-powerful One and please Him. The Bible says: "Therefore, whoever confesses Me before men, him I will also confess before My Father who is in heaven."[2]

I fear God in a healthy way. I know how proud the Father is of His Son. As a parent, I know how pleased my wife, Jane, and I are when someone says something nice about our children. Would God not have a similar response? Would He not be pleased to hear us acknowledge with honor the Name of His beloved Son? I want to please my Father in heaven no matter the cost.

I continued:

> We pray this in the name of the Father,
> And of the Son, the Lord Jesus Christ,
> And of the Holy Spirit. Amen.

To my surprise, I heard amens and applause from an audience assembled primarily for political interests—not religious. I was gratified that those listening had understood the importance of seeking God's favor. Upon returning to my seat, Senator Hillary Clinton, seated next to Tipper Gore, who sat next to Chelsea Clinton to my right, reached across these two ladies, clasped my hand, and whispered, "Thank you."

Able now to sit back and take in the remaining ceremony, I was proud of the president as he delivered an eloquent and power-filled speech and rejoiced with the ringing benediction given by Rev. Kirbyjon Caldwell. He did not hold anything back. He honored the Lord Jesus Christ and prayed in His Name.

After the swearing in, once again honoring the custom, the platform party followed President Bush and his family up the Capitol Building steps to the dome for the inaugural luncheon. Members of the Senate, the new cabinet, Supreme Court justices and their spouses were assembled. Just as my father had done four years earlier, I offered a prayer for the meal followed by heartwarming comments by President Bush to the distinguished guests. During the meal there was a steady stream of senators, both Democrat and Republican, who came to the head of the table to congratulate the new president. It is a day I will never forget, and I dare say most Americans will not forget either.

Jane and I were privileged to observe the inaugural parade down Pennsylvania Avenue from the president's viewing box. As the festivities were concluding, I slipped back to my hotel to put the final touches on my message to be delivered the next morning at the Cathedral. Most elected officials from the capitol city attended. This was specifically a religious service, the first such event sponsored by the new Bush White House. I felt complete freedom in the pulpit to say what I believed God had put in my heart.

After this service, I greeted the president and his family and assured him of my prayers as he shouldered such a heavy responsibility. That afternoon, following lunch with friends, I eagerly flew to a more serene atmosphere . . . home in the western mountains of North Carolina.

I thought I had left the inaugural flurry behind. However, days later, Alan Dershowitz, a man who described himself as a deeply committed Jew, took offense at my use of the Name of Jesus Christ. Dershowitz, a professor at Harvard Law School and an attorney who has defended clients as diverse as O. J. Simpson and Jim Bakker, in an opinion piece for the *Los Angeles Times*, said:

> The very first act of the new Bush administration was to have a Protestant Evangelical minister officially dedicate the inauguration to Jesus Christ, whom he declared to be "our savior." Invoking "the Father, the Son, the Lord Jesus Christ" and "the Holy Spirit," Billy Graham's son, the man selected by George W. Bush to bless his presidency, excluded the tens of millions of Americans who are Muslims, Jews, Buddhists, Shintoists, Unitarians, agnostics and atheists from his blessing by his particularistic and parochial language.

The entire article continued in the same venomous vein. Dershowitz did not disguise his outrage:

> It is permissible in the United States to reject any particular theology. Indeed that is part of our glorious diversity. What is not acceptable is for a presidential inauguration to exclude millions of citizens from its opening ceremony by dedicating it to a particular religious "savior."

The Dershowitz article concluded, "If Bush wants all Americans to accept him as their president, he made an inauspicious beginning by sandwiching his unity speech between two divisive, sectarian and inappropriate prayers."[3]

What was he talking about? I am a Christian. Don't ask me to pray like a Hindu; I am not a Hindu. Don't ask me to pray to Muhammad; I am not Muslim. I am a Christian. That is who I am: a believer in the greatest man that ever lived—Jesus Christ—a Jew.

The second prayer that Dershowitz referred to was, of course, the benediction prayed by Kirbyjon Caldwell in which he also had closed by invoking the Name of Jesus. Kirbyjon told *USA Today*, "I would have been misrepresenting who I am and arguably even why I was there had I not prayed in Jesus' name."[4]

Amen, Kirbyjon!

Alan Dershowitz should remember that this nation was built on a Christian foundation. Patrick Henry once declared, "It cannot be emphasized too strongly or too often that this great nation was founded, not by religionists, but by Christians; not on religions, but on the Gospel of Jesus Christ. For this very reason people of other faiths have been afforded asylum, prosperity, and freedom of worship here."[5]

I found Dershowitz's criticism galling. I had not excluded millions of Americans from my prayer. I wanted to ask Mr. Dershowitz, "Since I am a minister of the Gospel of the Lord Jesus Christ, if I am to express my religious freedom, how am I supposed to pray?" And who has the right to tell me what I should pray? As an American, am I not guaranteed freedom of speech? Freedom of worship? In my prayer, I did not ask or force anyone to agree with me. I did not suggest that the inaugural ceremony could not continue until everyone present "came forward to pray the sinner's prayer." I just did what I do: I always pray in His Name.

Others chimed in with Dershowitz. Barry Lynn, head of Americans United for the Separation of Church and State, said that both inaugural prayers were "inappropriate and insensitive." An article in the *New Republic* described the prayers that Kirbyjon and I offered as "crushing Christological thuds" that "barred millions of Americans from their own amens."[6]

I was not without defenders. I received hundreds of enthusiastic letters from individuals, and many in the media offered support. Jeff Jacoby, a columnist for the *Boston Globe*, wrote:

> Like it or not, American Jews—like American Muslims, Buddhists, Hindus, and atheists—are different from their neighbors.
>
> This country was founded by Christians and built on broad Christian principles. Threatening? Far from it: It is in precisely this Christian country that Jews have known the most peaceful, prosperous and successful existence in their long history.
>
> In America, a non-Christian need not answer "Amen" to an explicitly Christian prayer. This is a society where members of minority faiths live and worship without fear, secure in the hospitality and liberty America extends to all religions.
>
> No American should try to suppress the prayers of others. "Jesus" should not be a forbidden word in this land. Not even at a presidential inauguration.[7]

A letter written to the *Jewish Press* stated:

> No doubt any prayer would be offensive and exclusive to an atheist, but indulging such sensitivity would effectively give the non-believer a veto power over the free expression rights of the believer . . . I would expect a Christian minister who deeply believes in his faith to give a prayer grounded on that faith.[8]

The opinions expressed by some of those who reacted negatively should sound a loud warning bell to followers of Christ in America. For example, a student at Kent State University wrote, "Graham encourages us to acknowledge his God alone as our Lord, our Savior and our Redeemer."[9] He's exactly right. I do encourage everyone to acknowledge the one true God, and His Son and Him alone.

I cannot agree with the idea that every religious leader should be forced to pray "politically correct" prayers. Allowing someone to pray as he does normally in expressing his faith does not explicitly discount other religions. Think about this: If an atheist were invited to give the invocation at an inaugural—perish the thought—would we expect him to pray in the name of Jesus or any god?

I believe that the response to the inaugural prayers is additional evidence of a disturbing trend in American public life: Christians who use the Name of Jesus and insist that He is "the one and only way to God" are increasingly viewed by many in the liberal media as narrow-minded religious bigots who represent a threat to the rest of society.

Americans are extremely religious as the Gallup poll shows. But that religious bent rubs against another value in our society that may trump all others: tolerance. In our thirst for personal autonomy, the deal we seek is, "I will not question your beliefs or behavior if you will do the same for me." Does this now apply to spiritual issues too?

An eloquent advocate of Christian faith, Ravi Zacharias wrote in *Jesus Among Other Gods*,

> We are living in a time when angry voices demand with increasing insistence that we ought not to propagate the Gospel, that we ought not to consider anyone "lost" just because they are not Christians. "We are all born into different beliefs, and therefore, we should leave it that way"—so goes the tolerant "wisdom" of our time . . . When people make such statements, they forget or do not know that one is not born a Christian. All Christians are such by virtue of conversion. To ask the Christian not to reach out to anyone else who is from another faith is to ask that Christian to deny his own faith.[10]

None of this discussion and fuss really amounts to a hill of beans if Jesus Christ was just another "great teacher." But what if He is more than that? He is the One who said, "I am the way, the truth, and the life. No one comes to the Father except through Me."[11] A loyal follower of Jesus does not concoct personal ideas about these matters. All he or she does is faithfully represent the words of the Master. But this is increasingly considered suspect and even subversive in America.

Most "burning issues" in our day flame out quickly. Such was the case with the inaugural prayers. The media attention span is short, but at least for a few days in early 2001, the Name Jesus was heard in public discourse as something other than a curse word.

The bold reentry of the Name would not happen again for many months, until a shocking Tuesday morning in September.

4

WAR

You will never forget, nor will I.

The day Americans surrendered their innocence about their homeland's invincibility, I had watched the morning news and was about to leave for the office. Tuesday, September 11, 2001, was shaping up as a typically busy day.

The phone rang. "Have you seen what just happened?" a friend asked. Obviously, I had not. "Planes have flown into the World Trade Center," she said. Before I could gather my thoughts, she asked, "Will Edward have to go to war?" Our son Edward is a cadet at West Point. Before answering, I clicked on the television. As I watched the events unfold, there was no doubt in my mind that America would have to go to war. Within an hour or two of the attack, the towers imploded.

Like most Americans, I spent the rest of the day watching those pictures—over and over—of two passenger jets disappearing into the World Trade Center towers. I saw the smoke billowing from the Pentagon and wondered, *What's next? Will there be more attacks before this long day is over?*

The extent of the devastation was greater than the loss at Pearl Harbor. I knew the nation would soon be at war against evil. Not that we would do so to seek revenge, but to defend our very way of life. For too long Americans had seemed immune while France, Israel, South Africa, Russia, Bosnia, and Great Britain experienced terrorism. Now our own shores had been attacked in an attempt to destroy the heart of what our nation represents: economic, personal, and—above all—religious freedom.

Considering our opponents—individuals said to represent Islam—I knew a war driven by religious passions would not be as quick and direct as the Gulf War. I knew that this cowardly attack had at its heart great spiritual implications that would take this nation months, if not years, to understand. This war was really just another in a long history of battles related to the Name of the Lord Jesus Christ.

As that unforgettable week unfolded, reports surfaced that a national prayer service to honor the dead and seek God's mercy for America would be held in Washington, D.C., on Friday of that week. On Wednesday, September 12, my father was contacted by the White House and asked to deliver a message of comfort to the nation from Washington National Cathedral. I knew he was God's man for the moment. Many people view him as "America's Pastor," and felt he could bring comfort to our nation in crisis.

The next day, President Bush announced that we would observe a "national day of prayer and remembrance" on Friday.

Later that same day a producer at CNN called and asked if I would be willing to serve as a commentator for their live network coverage of the prayer service from the Cathedral. This was an interesting twist!

My assistant asked the producer if she was aware that Billy Graham would be speaking at the memorial service. The White House had not yet released the official list as to who would be participating in the prayer service; therefore, she had not heard that my father would bring the message. She began to cry. Her heart had been tenderized at the thought of my father sharing a message of comfort and hope and a son commenting on the event during this time of national tragedy. I accepted the invitation to appear on CNN's worldwide coverage of the service.

In times of unexpected crisis, fear and uncertainty overshadow hope. When a crisis is experienced by a nation everyone is affected. Biblical history illustrates that tragedy has a greater purpose than can be immediately seen. Daniel, the Hebrew prophet, wrote that the Most High God rules in the nations of earth, and is sovereign.[1] My hope as a minister of the Gospel was that I could use this platform as a commentator to bring hope and comfort in God's Name, for He is the "God of all comfort."[2]

There are many occasions when it is convenient to be a pilot, and September 13, 2001, was one of them. Most commercial airlines were grounded, as were all private aircraft. I was able to receive special permission from the Federal Department of Transportation and the FAA—arranged by the White House—to fly the Samaritan's Purse plane to Washington, D.C.

The flight through empty skies was the most eerie I have ever flown. Between North Carolina and the D.C. area, I did not see an airplane or hear a single radio transmission from another pilot. That does not happen in the busy airspace of the eastern United States. To me, this just underscored the crisis we were facing as a nation. Never before in our country's history had our entire airspace been closed. Making the approach to Dulles Airport from miles away, I saw the Pentagon bathed in bright lights as the rescue efforts continued. Dulles Airport was nearly deserted; just one plane rolled slowly down a taxiway.

That night at the hotel, I was once again glued to the TV screen. In reports from New York City, it was obvious that few if any additional survivors would be extricated from the World Trade Center rubble. I watched the heartbreaking sight of hundreds of relatives and friends wandering the streets, their faces contorted by fear and shock, searching for missing loved ones. Many of them displayed pictures and descriptions of family and friends, desperate for help.

Our ministry, Samaritan's Purse, is an evangelism, relief, and development organization that responds quickly to disasters and tragedies throughout the world in the Name of the Lord Jesus Christ. Often our first efforts involve medical assistance, providing food, shelter, and always sharing the hope we have in Christ. The situation in New York was different from the famine, flood, hurricane, civil war, or other disaster scenes we see so often. Though an adequate supply of volunteer doctors, nurses, and emergency personnel were on hand, and hospitals were on alert, few victims were recovered in time to save their lives. Other services provided by our disaster response team were not needed. Instead of wrecked homes or villages, here were New York's tallest buildings lying in a heap on the ground. Clearing this rubble required special equipment and training that we did not have.

New York also needed another kind of help. My heart was touched by the sight of New Yorkers of different races and backgrounds reaching out to each other. As I watched grief-stricken faces in desperation, people holding up signs, drifting from hospital to hospital in frantic search for lost loved ones, the Lord placed an idea in my heart. Perhaps what New Yorkers needed even more was immediate spiritual help.

Immediately I called our project director at Samaritan's Purse. We discussed some options. "This is different from a flood or an earthquake," I told him. "I want you to go to New York City and find a building where we can open a prayer center, a place where these hurting family members and others can drop in or call to get spiritual help—offer them some hope. Let's recruit pastors and Christian workers and send them in teams to the city. They can take to the streets, meet people and offer to pray with them right there."

"I'll get right on it," he answered. With years of experience in overcoming obstacles in "impossible" situations, I knew this would be a special challenge and it would not be long before he reported that a prayer center would open in the heart of Manhattan.

A MEMORABLE MEMORIAL SERVICE

At 10 A.M. on September 14, I arrived at the majestic Cathedral in Washington, D.C. The weather was miserable, a steady drizzle dripping from a low, gray sky. The wet gloom seemed a match for the nation's mood. The reporter assigned by CNN was their Washington correspondent, Judy Woodruff. She and I would use CNN's outdoor "set" in front of the Cathedral steps. We had plenty of company. The space assigned to the media was jammed with representatives from every major news organization in the world. I was thankful that our president had scheduled this historic service. Our nation needed to seek God's face at this hour. The entire viewing world would now see America calling out to God in prayer, seeking His mercy and comfort during this national crisis. What a testimony this could be to the entire world.

CNN's coverage began at 11 A.M. Before long, a host of political dignitaries began flowing into the Cathedral. Judy and I observed the guests taking their seats via a tiny monitor. Raindrops splashed on our heads as gusts of wind whipped through the open sides of our temporary shelter.

Between reports about what was happening at the Cathedral and elsewhere as the country and world paused to pray for the families and victims of this tragedy, Judy questioned me about what the "Christian response" should be to these acts of terrorism. My desire is to always emphasize the Gospel—the only hope for the world—urging viewers not to turn bitter in the face of such evil.

I recalled the story of King David in Old Testament times. He fought forcefully against the enemies of God. It was appropriate and necessary that the United States defend itself and use its might as a super power to defeat the enemies of our nation. I was moved by the privilege God had given me to bring a biblical perspective on live worldwide television.

As individuals, we must not let our hearts harden. I reminded those listening that many people in the Muslim/Arab world were sickened by the tragedy and not at all in agreement with the twisted ideas of the radical Islamic perpetrators.

As Judy and I discussed the week's events, dignitaries continued to arrive, one limousine after another. Faces were sad but resolute. Tiny red, white, and blue lapel ribbons were visible emblems commemorating the lost.

Judy Woodruff commented: "We all want to believe at this time that there is someone who can bring us salvation." What a remarkable statement. It speaks to the hunger the world has to find refuge in times of trouble. I responded with the Gospel and the hope that we have in Jesus Christ.

In answer to more of reporter Woodruff's questions, I also admitted that I did not have a full understanding of why God would allow such a massacre of innocent life. Based on what Paul wrote in his second letter to the Thessalonians, we know that a "mystery of lawlessness is already at work."[3]

The Devil has power on earth, but it is limited. He is not omnipresent, he is not omniscient, but he does have demons under his authority. The Bible tells us that Satan seeks to devour and destroy. Many times when tragedies occur people often ask: Why did God allow this? It was never God's plan and purpose on earth for man to live with sin and its consequences, but because of man's disobedience, sin came into the world.

We live in a world filled with evil and contaminated by sin. Although we are shocked by tragedies, despicable and heinous acts should not surprise us as much as they do. Without the redeeming power of God, the human heart is a sewer of sinful desires and schemes. As Jesus once said, "A good man out of the good treasure of his heart brings forth good things, and an evil man out of the evil treasure brings forth evil things."[4]

Government officials arrived at the Cathedral, along with the former living presidents and their wives (except for Ronald and Nancy Reagan). Just as the service was about to begin, the rain stopped. Rays of sunlight pierced through a gray sky. A sign of hope seemed to break through after such a grim week of horror and death; beyond the clouds the sky was bright and blue. The brilliance of God's hope is always present if we will just look up.

At noon, as the service began, church bells rang throughout the country—and even in many foreign nations—as millions gathered to pray and remember the dead. Many businesses allowed employees to leave work so they could attend services. In an interview aired on

CNN, former U.S. Secretary of Education Bill Bennett said it so well: "We pray today; we fight tomorrow."[5] And fight tomorrow we did.

The service was outstanding, a moving and inspiring mix of music and well-chosen words in prayers and speeches. Representatives of several faiths participated, including Rev. Kirbyjon Caldwell, who read Scripture and prayed.

The time came for my father to speak. Though he needed some assistance to maneuver the steps, I was so proud of him when he took hold of the pulpit. In spite of his eighty-two years, his strong and bold voice commanded attention, and the millions that listened around the world—in nearly every nation on earth—heard words of comfort found in the hope only Jesus Christ can give. It has been said that this was the only time in history that the Gospel was presented to so many people at one time. As Scripture teaches, God can take the most difficult trials in life and use them for good. The terrorists struck at America on behalf of their "god." They had intended evil. But God Almighty used this tragic event to send healing and comfort through the Good News of His Son throughout the world.

As a respectful hush fell across that great Cathedral, my father began his message acknowledging Almighty God.

> Today we come together in this service to confess our need of God. We have always needed God from the very beginning of this nation. But today we need Him especially. We are involved in a new kind of warfare and need the help of the Spirit of God . . . But how do we understand something like this? Why does God allow evil like this to take place? First, we are reminded of the mystery and reality of evil . . . I have to confess that I do not know the answer. I have to accept, by faith, that God is sovereign, and that He is a God of love and mercy and compassion in the midst of suffering. The Bible says God is not the Author of evil . . .
>
> Here in this majestic National Cathedral we see all around us the symbol of the cross. For the Christian, the cross tells us that God understands our sin and our suffering, for He took them upon Himself in the Person of Jesus Christ. From the cross God declared

> His love for us. He knows our heartaches, our sorrows, and pain that we feel.
>
> The story does not end with the cross, for Easter points us beyond the tragedy of the cross to the empty tomb. It tells us that there is hope for eternal life, for Christ has conquered evil, death, and hell . . .
>
> This week we watched in horror as planes crashed into the steel and glass of the World Trade Center. Those majestic towers, built on solid foundations, were examples of prosperity and creativity. When damaged, those buildings plummeted to the ground, imploding in upon them. Yet, underneath the debris, is a foundation that was not destroyed . . . Yes, our nation has been attacked, buildings destroyed, lives lost. Now we have a choice: whether to implode and disintegrate emotionally and spiritually as a people and a nation; or to choose to become stronger through this struggle, to rebuild on a solid foundation.

When my father finished, a spontaneous ovation took place as those in the Cathedral rose to their feet in honor of a man and the message he has been so faithful to proclaim for half a century. As Judy and I watched from outside she said, "They are clapping for your father!" She later told me how that had moved her heart. As President Bush made his way to the platform, all listened with anticipation to one of the greatest speeches given by a president in modern times. "This nation is peaceful, but fierce when stirred to anger," the president said. "This conflict was begun on the timing and terms of others. It will end in a way and at an hour of our choosing."

I appreciated so much President Bush's frequent references to God and our need as a nation to trust in Him. How refreshing to see our president and the leader of the free world leading us to prayer.

President Bush declared with passion, "Our responsibility to history is already clear, to answer these attacks and rid the world of evil."

What a noble endeavor. Of course, evil will not disappear even if we see the end of Osama bin Laden's influence and every Al Qaeda member behind bars. The demise of the Taliban in Afghanistan will not crush all evil in Afghanistan. If all wicked governments and their leaders fell, evil would still exist because it is nurtured in the human heart.

The battle America is fighting against terrorism is really just a skirmish in a war that began when Satan turned against God and made his declaration of independence. God sent His Son to this earth on the ultimate commando raid. As my father said in his sermon at the Cathedral, Jesus won the victory for us on the cross. The Apostle John wrote: "He who sins is of the devil, for the devil has sinned from the beginning. For this purpose the Son of God was manifested, that He might destroy the works of the devil."[6] God inflicted the deathblow to evil on the cross, but the "mop-up" operation will continue until He returns.

At the conclusion of the memorial service, in the warmth of the welcome sun, I headed back to Dulles International, boarded the plane, and returned home. This was definitely not a time I wanted to hang around our nation's capital, a city that looked like it was under siege—National Guard troops patrolled the streets. Washington was still in the sites of hostile forces. Were terrorists planning additional attacks? I was glad to be heading south. The Blue Ridge Mountains seemed now a refuge from the gales of our national storm.

THE GOSPEL TRIUMPHS AT HOME AND ABROAD

Once again, the Samaritan's Purse team did superb work. This time we teamed up with the Billy Graham Evangelistic Association (BGEA), and the following week we were able to open the "Billy Graham Prayer Center" in Manhattan. Office space was secured with little trouble. However, we ran into a major glitch when the phone company learned that we were requesting multiple phone lines to be installed. Their representative almost laughed. Because of the chaos in the city, he estimated it would take six months to do the work.

My project director did not take "no" as an acceptable response. He began to explain the purpose of the center. It was not until he mentioned my father's name, however, that the company's representative changed his response. When the name "Billy Graham" was mentioned, he assured my director they would do their best. The next day the phone lines were installed and we were officially up and running. What political clout or money cannot secure, the power of a name often can.

What made the man from the phone company change his estimate from six months to "right away"? It appears that my father's name opened the way. Years of faithful ministry and unwavering integrity in representing the Name of Jesus Christ have given my father respect by both believers and nonbelievers. It sure helped to open doors in New York City because soon our ministry teams were on the streets, seeking individuals in need, offering to pray with them. Some of those who called our hot line talked for hours at a time. People were hungry spiritually and crying out for hope.

We received reports from other countries where friends had witnessed remarkable responses to my father's message at the Cathedral. One of these came from an American half the world away in Malaysia. The only place with a television that carried CNN happened to be in a bar, so in order to keep up with the events, that's where he headed. A portion of his message read:

> While I have not been able to follow all the news coverage of the events in the U.S. I did find a pub or bar next door to my hotel which had CNN . . . Two nights ago, I was sitting on a bar stool watching the National Prayer Service in the Washington Cathedral. The Chinese and Indian drinkers around me had had a little too much to drink causing their voices to get increasingly louder . . . making it nearly impossible to hear the volume on the TV. But suddenly the most amazing thing happened. When Billy Graham was helped up the stairs to the podium, everyone in the bar fell silent. Every Buddhist, Hindu and Muslim in the place sat spellbound as they listened to the Gospel being presented. I never have associated bars with the presence of God's Spirit. But the sense of His presence in that little bar in Klang, Malaysia, was so strong I caught myself wiping tears from my eyes . . .
>
> As the Lord's Prayer was sung, the TV camera panned to the cross and there was Jesus for the entire world to see. Even those of

> us in a little bar in Klang, Malaysia, witnessed Jesus being lifted up. Now my prayer is that all people will be drawn to Him.[7]

We heard many testimonies about the impact the memorial service had also made on New Yorkers. I paid a visit to New York City the first week of October and Deputy Mayor Rudy Washington spent several hours showing me Ground Zero and the surrounding neighborhoods. Even three weeks after the attack, the sights and smells of the devastation were overwhelming. Almost everyone I spoke with still seemed dazed. I have witnessed destruction and devastation in places like the Middle East and Africa, but I do not ever recall seeing such shock and spiritual hunger in the eyes of Americans.

Although terrorists acting of their own free will attacked America on September 11, they are just pawns in a chess war as big as the universe that encompasses the ages. Our nation is full of problems and much in need of repentance from sin. As imperfect a model as we are, America, at its core, is a symbol of the freedom purchased with the precious blood of the Lord Jesus on the Cross—the freedom of men and women to choose to love and follow the Savior of their souls, to align themselves with the Name.

We must realize that there is a war under way that is much bigger than terrorists' attacks. This is a war that transcends politics and religion. The real battle going on today is between good and evil, God and Satan. In every culture, in every nation, in every state, city, and community, in every home, and ultimately in every heart, a war rages on.

This truly is a "holy war" . . . over the Name.

5

WHERE'S THE TOLERANCE?

Tolerance has become the new watchword of our times. It is heralded as perhaps the highest virtue in Western culture that glues people of differing backgrounds and ideologies together for the sake of promoting cultural unity. And why shouldn't it be? It sounds good, right? In fact, it sounds so good that anyone who would dare talk negatively about this sacred cow of civility would almost be considered immoral. But that's just the point. The media and the governmental bureaucrats tell us to be tolerant of everything and anything except the Gospel of salvation, all in the name of political correctness. It seems almost ironic that Christians are not being tolerated by such a "tolerant" society.

So I admit, I get frustrated and a bit defensive when I encounter intolerance toward the Name of the Lord Jesus Christ. In Western societies these days, just about any viewpoint, religion, or behavior is exempt from criticism in the name of "tolerance." It is "politically incorrect" to give anything but reverent respect to the most off-the-wall ideas that come from individuals. All of this is done in the name of "tolerance."

But such tolerance is not universal. One of the few loopholes in the "law of tolerance" involves followers of the Name of Jesus Christ. If you are a born-again Christian, don't expect the same tolerance that others enjoy—the playing field is not level as it relates to other beliefs. For decades now, Christians have been on the run over issues like prayer in public forums and Nativity scenes erected on public property. Even Christmas is being altered to such euphemisms as "Season's Greetings" and "Happy Holidays." But such aggressive opposition to the insertion of the Christian faith into the secular arena has not been brought against other religions.

To illustrate: Since the September 11 attacks, there has been heightened interest in America concerning Islam. For instance, one California school district went so far as to require seventh-grade students to learn the tenets of Islam, study important persons in the history of the religion, learn verses from the Koran, pray "in the name of Allah, the Compassionate, the Merciful," and chant "Praise to Allah, Lord of Creation."[1]

Can you imagine the lawsuits that would raise their ugly heads if a teacher commanded students to memorize Bible verses, recite the Lord's Prayer, or pray in the Name of Jesus? Any teacher that would allow this would be fired, and the school sued!

Youth speaker Josh McDowell comments on the trend this way:

> What happens when your child is taught that his beliefs and values are no different from a Buddhist's—or a homosexual—or someone involved in pre-marital sex? This is today's tolerance. And it's the number one virtue in America, especially among our youth. Our kids are being taught that all truth is relative to the individual. Knowing Right from Wrong doesn't matter. To say something is right or wrong is not being tolerant. God never once in the Bible calls us to be tolerant. Our children are not called to be tolerant. Rather, He calls us to act justly and to be loving.[2]

Christians are increasingly not tolerated because they are viewed as intolerant! I agree wholeheartedly with my friend Christian apologist

Ravi Zacharias, who wrote in *Jesus Among Other Gods:*

> We are living in a time when sensitivities are at the surface, often vented in cutting words. Philosophically, you can practice anything, so long as you do not claim that it is a "better" way. Religiously, you can hold to anything, so long as you do not bring Jesus Christ into it. If a spiritual idea is eastern, it is granted critical immunity; if western, it is thoroughly criticized . . . All religions, plainly and simply, cannot be true . . . It does no good to put a halo on the notion of tolerance as if everything could be equally true.[3]

In the past, "tolerance" in matters of faith meant respectful acknowledgment of different ideas. It did not mean that all such ideas were granted equal validity as truth. It makes me wonder why other religions are able to promote their theology in public forums. Even our government seems to bend over backward to give them a hearing. But these days if you mention the Name of Jesus or seek to discuss Christian ideas publicly, you risk being labeled by the media-created term "the religious right" and are considered a dangerous threat to the doctrine of the separation of church and state.

Focus on the Family did an in-depth investigation on this issue of "church and state" separation. In its *Citizen* magazine they reported:

> An FBI analysis shows that Thomas Jefferson's views on church and state weren't what we've heard—far from it. When Thomas Jefferson penned his now famous phrase, "a wall of separation between Church and State," in a letter dated January 1, 1802, to the Danbury Baptist Association in Connecticut, did he expect it to be memorable?
>
> Maybe.
>
> A 1998 FBI laboratory analysis of the letter showed that Jefferson labored over that portion of his letter, perhaps fussing over its political impact. But did our third president expect his words to effectively drive religion out of the public square?
>
> No . . .

> Jefferson's initial draft reveals his understanding that the federal government simply lacked jurisdiction over religion.
>
> So who gave us the wall of separation that renders prayers at graduations and in public parks unconstitutional? The author of that wall was not Jefferson, but U.S. Supreme Court Justice Hugo Black, appointed by Franklin Roosevelt in 1937 and who served until his death in 1971. In a number of rulings he helped write, Black used Jefferson's language, but not Jefferson's meaning.
>
> Black's separationist leanings became more aggressive over time, resulting in rulings that ordered the removal of religious instruction, prayer and Bible reading from public schools and bans on graduation prayers and the posting of the Ten Commandments.[4]

Other historic writers have made further note of Jefferson's intentions:

> One of his [Thomas Jefferson's] greatest achievements was the passage of the Virginia Statute of Religious Liberty, which was passed in 1786 after a long and heated debate in the legislature. This piece of legislation provided the basis for the constitutional guarantee of religious freedom as found in the First Amendment of the Constitution . . . Jefferson's wish had been turned into law: "An Act for Establishing Religious Freedom . . . that all men shall be free to profess, and by argument to maintain, their opinion in matters of religion, and that the same shall in no wise diminish, enlarge, or affect their civil capacities."[5]

The painful irony is that it was our Christian roots in America that created an environment supportive of free thought and behavior that has resulted in tolerance, as it is now understood. Regardless of what the media movers and shakers think about Christians, the truth remains that their very freedom to express such opinions is a result of this nation's Christian heritage. Our democratic system did not spring from Hindu, Buddhist, Shinto, or Moslem traditions. The Bible—not the Koran, Vedas, Tripitika, or other so-called holy books—is the source of our nation's philosophy on the value of mankind and how they should treat one another and be governed. Even today, men and women are laying down their lives to preserve our Bible-based freedom.

A few months after the September 11 attacks on our nation, I met Shannon Spann, the young widow of CIA agent Mike Spann, who was the first American to die by hostile action in Afghanistan. Shannon told me that she and her husband were both believers in Christ and that Mike gladly put his life on the line—and ultimately gave it for his country—because of his conviction that the freedom America offers to proclaim one's faith had to be protected. His courage, and that of others like him, was different from the mealymouthed idea of tolerance that is talked about so much these days.

Yet in its programming, the entertainment industry depicts ministers and Christians as sexual perverts, swindlers, thieves, murderers, drunkards, and morally weak individuals who rarely take a stand and appear to be wishy-washy on doctrines of the faith. Are there ministers that have been guilty of these things? Yes. But there are hundreds of thousands of ministers who have been faithful to their calling, who have never been involved in scandals or sordid relationships, but have honorably served their churches and communities year in and year out. Where is the mention of these faithful ones? Does the popular press talk about them?

America is infatuated with this false understanding of tolerance. To be truly tolerant is *not* to give every idea equal standing or to compromise the truth in the interest of keeping the peace and making everyone happy. Being tolerant *does* mean accepting the fact that every person is created in the image of Almighty God and that we each have a soul that will live for eternity. Jesus Christ paid the price for our eternal salvation through the shedding of His blood on Calvary's cross for all men—equally.

In America, we often take for granted our constitutional system and assume that tolerance of different religions is true everywhere. Not so! No doubt I am especially aware of this issue because I have seen firsthand what life is like in other countries where the dominant point of view is not founded and based upon the Holy Bible.

A PERSONAL EXPERIENCE

The greatest act of tolerance in all of human history was the death and resurrection of God's Son, Jesus Christ. It was not exclusive for one class or another, for one race or another, but for all.

That is why at Samaritan's Purse we commit ourselves to expressing God's tolerance shown through His unconditional love and His grace and mercy to some of the most devastated people on earth.

We have worked since the early 1990s to relieve some of the pain and suffering of people living in the southern part of Sudan and have opened up a hospital there. Many Americans are unaware that since 1986, the current Islamic government of this African nation has overseen the annihilation of more than two million southern Sudanese. Long before the events of 9/11 that shook the very heart and soul of this nation, I learned firsthand how some followers of Islam express their faith.

Approximately twenty-two miles east of our hospital in Lui, in southern Sudan, lies the front line of the war. It is at a place called Rokon. In Rokon, there is a small riverbed where a one-lane bridge covers the span. It is at this bridge and riverbed that the front line of the war is drawn. The riverbed and the low-lying areas on both sides of it are full of human skeletons, many of them still in the remnants of the uniforms and the clothes in which the men and civilians on both sides of the conflict died.

When it took power, this radical Islamic government mandated that the entire country must live under the Islamic law. Millions of southern Sudanese, which are predominantly Christian, decided that they were not going to be forced to bow to the god of Islam or to live under its laws and mandates.

This bold stand for religious freedom prompted what has become Africa's longest and bloodiest civil war—a war not so much political but religious in nature. These brave Christians would rather risk eradication than have their children forced to attend Islamic schools and undergo Islamic indoctrination including reading, memorizing, and reciting the Koran.

Americans should understand their longings: Our early forefathers came to America's shores not to find political freedom per se, but to be free to worship God in their own way. The United States was built upon the principles of men and women willing to die for religious freedom. The Pilgrims who landed at Plymouth Rock wanted to worship God without government interference. Likewise, the southern Sudanese do not necessarily want to establish their own nation; they want to be good citizens of their country. They are God-fearing people who are not Muslim and do not want to be forced into Islam. They want their freedom—freedom to have their own schools, freedom to worship God based upon instruction found in the Bible. To a large extent, it is a battle of distinctly different ideas about how humanity should live. It is Islam against Christianity—and Islam against everybody else. It is also this Muslim government that allows slavery. Today, in the Sudan, black Africans are still bought and sold in slave markets in the name of Islam.

The Islamic government of Sudan has purposely targeted Christians and minorities of other faiths. "Ethnic cleansing" has forced millions to leave their homes and land, fleeing for their lives. The stories of atrocities are all too familiar: women raped; children, women, and young men abducted into slavery by government militias; ruthless amputations; pastors crucified. Our relief workers have seen burned-out villages, mutilated bodies, destruction of homes and the targeting of schools, churches, and hospitals.

John Deng James, a young boy caught in a fiery battle that raged through a Sudanese village, found himself alone in his uncle's pool of blood. He and many other young children fled, walking for days, then weeks, and finally months before realizing that they would never return home or see their families again. These boys belong to a group referred to by international aid organizations as the "Lost Boys of Sudan." Some twenty-six thousand Sudanese boys were forced by violence from their southern Sudan villages in the late 1980s.

According to the U.S. State Department estimates, the combination of war, famine, and disease in southern Sudan has killed more than two million people and displaced another four million.[6]

Sadly, much of the world has all but forgotten the cry of agony rising from black Africans of southern Sudan. Although the media in America normally do not report on this conflict, of late we have heard more about Sudan because of its support of international terrorism. In the early 1990s it was home to Osama bin Laden and numerous other international terrorists. You may recall that on August 20, 1998, the United States attacked a Khartoum facility, known as the Shifa factory, suspected of manufacturing precursors to chemical agents intended for biological warfare. This was in retaliation for the bombing of the U.S. Embassies in Kenya and Tanzania.

Providentially, I was visiting Sudan just before this incident. Samaritan's Purse had opened what was to become one of the largest hospitals in the southern Sudan, the area where the SPLA (Sudan People's Liberation Army) has resisted the Islamic government. The need for medical care was so great that people were walking from as far as one hundred miles away to receive treatment. Since this hospital opened, more than one hundred thousand Sudanese have received medical assistance. We also have been able to airlift into the country tons of seed, chickens, farm tools, and other supplies to give the people the resources required to reverse the results of a consuming famine, which is caused primarily by the war of aggression by the Islamic government.

Because roads are mined and bridges have been blown up, supply convoys by road are almost impossible. Basically, the only way in and out is by air. Our planes, which are subject to the threat of attack, must fly hundreds of miles from bases in Kenya.

In the year 2000, the Sudanese government started an air bombing campaign intended to wipe out any infrastructure of public services in the non-Muslim-controlled areas. Bombs fell on hospitals, schools, food distribution centers, churches and civilian areas; no civilian target was off-limits. Apparently, this terrorist government wanted to terrorize and strike fear in the people. Believe me, when the bombs hit, it worked. More than three dozen bombs hit the area where our hospital is located. Miraculously, the hospital building was not badly damaged, and the fatalities and casualties in the adjacent village were light, compared to what could have been.

These southern Sudanese believers are unfazed. Years ago they could have succumbed to living under Islamic law as non-Muslims and second-class citizens, but even then they would have faced persecution. The Islamic government would have forced their children to attend Muslim schools for indoctrination. Instead of bowing to their demands, these Sudanese Christians decided to fight for freedom, choosing deprivation and suffering in order to worship God freely and follow the Lord Jesus Christ.

Over the years I have had the opportunity to work in many Muslim countries, including Egypt, Jordan, Lebanon, Syria, Iraq, Afghanistan, Pakistan, as well as Sudan. In some Islamic countries, such as Saudi Arabia for example, there is not one Christian church. To my knowledge Afghanistan, which the United States liberated from the Taliban and whose people have been freed, does not have a single church building. This was not always true.

In 1959 an American Christian missionary serving in Afghanistan, Dr. J. Christy Wilson Jr., contacted President Dwight Eisenhower to seek his help in obtaining permission from the government of Afghanistan to build a church in Kabul. Dr. Wilson pointed out that a Muslim mosque had been built in Washington, D.C. When President Eisenhower visited Afghanistan the same year, he asked permission from the Afghan king, and received approval, for a church to be built. Years passed, but finally in 1970 the church building was finished and dedicated.

Just three years later the Muslim government began hunting Christians. Dr. Wilson, his wife, Betty, and others, who had done so much for the Afghan people, were ordered out of the country. The government decided to tear down the church. In spite of pleas from many influential Christians around the world, the king did not intervene, and the building was leveled on July 17, 1973. That very night the king was deposed in a military coup.

Afghan refugees later told Dr.Wilson, "Ever since our government destroyed that Christian church, God has been judging our country."[7] I don't know if this is the reason for Afghan's troubled times, but the facts are clear: Afghanistan has known war, horrible poverty, and suffering almost without ceasing since the 1970s. Perhaps now, by God's mercy, with the end of the Taliban, the Afghan people will once again have the opportunity to hear and embrace the truth of the Gospel.

My point is, in America we have enjoyed more than two hundred years of freedom, abundance, and unprecedented progress because our system reflects the teaching of the greatest Book ever written and the greatest Teacher who ever lived. Why, then, are Christians in America increasingly finding themselves under accusation, attack, and even the first stages of persecution?

THE NAME DIVIDES

Christians must not forget their identity; Christians are first and foremost citizens of the Kingdom of Heaven. Whether or not we are treated well in America or anywhere else is not our primary concern. Identifying with Jesus Christ and His cause will bring trouble and even persecution from the people of the world. Jesus promised that this would happen:

> Blessed are you when men hate you,
> And when they exclude you,
> And revile you, and cast out your name as evil,
> For the Son of Man's sake . . .
> For indeed your reward is great in heaven.[8]

And on another occasion, Jesus said to His disciples as He sent them throughout Israel:

> "Do not go into the way of the Gentiles, and do not enter a city of the Samaritans. But go rather to the lost sheep of the house of Israel. And as you go, preach, saying, 'The kingdom of heaven is at hand.' Heal the sick, cleanse the lepers, raise the dead, cast out demons . . . Behold, I send you out as sheep in the midst of wolves. Therefore be wise as serpents and harmless as doves. But beware of men, for they will deliver you up to councils and

> scourge you in their synagogues. You will be brought before governors and kings for My sake."[9]

Those are sobering words. As American citizens, Christians have the same constitutional rights as everyone else. I am offended when others display intolerance when I take my stand for Jesus Christ. Such prejudice should not totally surprise me either. The Lord Jesus Christ warns that His followers cannot avoid being hated for His "name's sake."

The Name of Jesus Christ is a lightning rod because Jesus Christ represents the division of life between good and evil, God and Satan, light and darkness, righteousness and sin, heaven and hell. The Name of Jesus shouts out a choice: "Whom will you serve, give your life to, depend upon?" Rebellious, self-willed, sinful people want to retain the right to decide for themselves which way they will take. Jesus denies this option. Speaking on His behalf, the Apostle Peter said, "For there is no other name under heaven given among men by which we must be saved."[10]

Jesus is gentle, but He is not weak. He loves the sinner but is absolutely intolerant of sin. He is not a negotiator. He is Lord.

It is this bristling truth that invites intolerance toward Christians. Jesus did not say, "Do your own thing; all roads lead to God." That would have made Jesus "politically correct," but Jesus is not politically correct. He is Lord.

His followers today must accept the eternal truth of what He said to His disciples:

> If the world hates you, you know that it hated Me before it hated you. If you were of the world, the world would love its own. Yet because you are not of the world, but I chose you out of the world, therefore the world hates you. Remember the word that I said to you, "A servant is not greater than his master." If they persecuted Me, they will also persecute you. If they kept My word, they will keep yours also. But all these things they will do to you for My name's sake, because they do not know Him who sent Me.[11]

THE TOLERANCE OF JESUS

Jesus was wonderfully tolerant in the way He dealt with people as we see when He met the woman of Samaria. Jews during this time had little to do with the despised Samaritans. But Jesus did not participate in what would have been "politically correct" racial or sexual prejudice. He was compassionate and tolerant toward the sinner but knew how to draw a line when it came to the sinfulness in a person's life. A story in the book of John vividly illustrates this:

> So He [Jesus] came to a city of Samaria which is called Sychar, near the plot of ground that Jacob gave to his son Joseph. Now Jacob's well was there. Jesus therefore, being wearied form His journey, sat thus by the well. It was about the sixth hour. A woman of Samaria came to draw water. Jesus said to her, "Give Me a drink." For His disciples had gone away into the city to buy food. Then the woman of Samaria said to Him, "How is it that You, being a Jew, ask a drink from me, a Samaritan woman?" For Jews have no dealings with Samaritans. Jesus answered and said to her, "If you knew the gift of God, and who it is who says to you, 'Give Me a drink,' you would have asked Him, and He would have given you living water." The woman said to Him, "Sir, You have nothing to draw with, and the well is deep. Where then do You get that living water? Are You greater than our father Jacob, who gave us the well, and drank from it himself, as well as his sons and his livestock?" Jesus answered and said to her, "Whoever drinks of this water will thirst again, but whoever drinks of the water that I shall give him will never thirst. But the water that I shall give him will become in him a fountain of water springing up into everlasting life." The woman said to Him, "Sir, give me this water, that I may not thirst, nor come here to draw." Jesus said to her, "Go, call your husband, and come here." The woman answered and said, "I have no husband." Jesus said to her, "You have well said, 'I have no husband,' for you have had five husbands, and the one whom you now have is not your husband; in that you spoke

> truly." The woman said to Him, "Sir, I perceive that You are a prophet. Our fathers worshiped on this mountain, and you Jews say that in Jerusalem is the place where one ought to worship." Jesus said to her, "Woman, believe Me, the hour is coming when you will neither on this mountain, nor in Jerusalem, worship the Father. You worship what you do not know; we know what we worship, for salvation is of the Jews. But the hour is coming and now is, when the true worshipers will worship the Father in spirit and truth; for the Father is seeking such to worship Him. God is Spirit, and those who worship Him must worship in spirit and truth." The woman said to Him, "I know that Messiah is coming" (who is called Christ). "When He comes, He will tell us all things." Jesus said to her, "I who speak to you am He."[12]

Jesus spoke with compassion and understanding, and He explained to her spiritual truths so well so that she left her water pot and went into the city and told the men what had happened and much of the city came to meet Jesus.

During His ministry on earth, many pagan religions vied for the hearts and minds of people. Jesus' followers assumed He would want to squelch those who did not agree with Him. But instead, Jesus was tolerant and dealt with those of other faiths in kindness and love. Here was a woman obviously living a sinful life, trapped by religious tradition, and spiritual blindness; yet Jesus dealt with her delicately.

Jesus could be tough at times with the Jewish Pharisees and even His own disciples. In one of His parables, Jesus told how Satan had sowed tares or weeds in a field planted with wheat. When the sprouts came forth from the earth, the field was full of both wheat and weeds. But the owner of the field did not let his workers go and pull out the weeds. Instead he told them to let everything grow. After the harvest, then the weeds would be separated from the grain.[13]

The point Jesus was making was to let the false teachers and the religions they follow grow; they were not to persecute or force anyone into His kingdom, they were not to violate people's freedom to choose. Jesus invites all to come to Him, but it is an individual choice to accept or reject Christ. When the harvest (which represents the end of time) comes, Jesus will separate the thousands of false believers (the tares) from those who followed Him (the wheat).

History records that there have been rulers and kings in the past who have disobeyed God's Word and have manipulated and twisted God's truth for their own political purposes, such as the crusaders during medieval times who carried the cross of Christ and massacred Muslims and Jews alike. Nowhere in the Bible is that supported by the teachings of Christ.

Must we tolerate those who think Christians are ignorant, foolish, and intolerant? This is the attitude Jesus wants to find in us:

> You have heard that it was said, "An eye for an eye and a tooth for a tooth." But I tell you not to resist an evil person. But whoever slaps you on your right cheek, turn the other to him also . . .
>
> You have heard that it was said, "You shall love your neighbor and hate your enemy." But I say to you, love your enemies, bless those who curse you, do good to those who hate you, and pray for those who spitefully use you and persecute you, that you may be sons of your Father in heaven; for He makes His sun rise on the evil and on the good, and sends rain on the just and on the unjust.[14]

As an American citizen, I have the right to believe as I see fit regardless of what is politically correct. Those who seek to suppress the principles of Christian faith do not realize their peril. A visit to countries where governments are under the influence of other religions will reveal just how precious our core freedoms are here in America.

God is not tolerant of sin or other religions that lead people into everlasting darkness. The Bible says that there will be a judgment at the appointed time; for He is a jealous God, and clearly there should be no other gods before Him.[15]

But in the meantime, this fad of tolerance—which is intolerant of defenders of the Name—has my stomach churning.

As a follower of Jesus Christ I have to confess that I long for a homeland that's far better and more enduring than what the world has to offer. Like the men and women mentioned in the book of Hebrews, I am a stranger and pilgrim on this earth, seeking a "heavenly country" whose maker and builder is God.[16]

6

ABOVE OTHER "GODS"

How many religions would you guess there are in the world? Fifty? One hundred? One thousand? Five thousand?

The major ones include Christianity, Judaism, Islam, Hinduism, Buddhism, and Shintoism. David Barrett, the editor of the *World Christian Encyclopedia*, stated that there are 9,900 distinct and separate religions in the world.[1] And it increases every year!

How, then, is it possible for Christians to be so confident about the preeminence of Jesus Christ? Why can't Christians just be content to say that Jesus was simply a good teacher of the past, someone to point the way to God just like so many other religious leaders before and after Him?

The answer about the supreme truth of Christianity revolves around the One who bears the Name—the Lord Jesus Christ. C. S. Lewis, renowned British thinker and writer and one of history's greatest defenders of the Christian faith, wrote:

> A man who was merely a man and said the sort of things Jesus said would not be a great moral teacher. He would either be a lunatic—

> level with the man who says he is a poached egg—or else he d be the Devil of Hell. You must make your choice. Either this man was, and is, the Son of God: or else a madman or something worse. You can shut Him up for a fool, you can spit at Him and kill Him as a Demon; or you can fall at His feet and call Him Lord and God. But let us not come with any patronizing nonsense about His being a great human teacher. He has not left that open to us. He did not intend to.[2]

Lewis insightfully pointed out that Jesus couldn't be merely a "good teacher," given what He claimed about Himself in what history records about Him. That option simply isn't available to any thinking person.

But is Jesus the only way to God?

This question has received renewed attention in the wake of the September 11 attacks on the World Trade Center and the Pentagon, because the planners and perpetrators of those wicked deeds were followers of Islam.

As I write these words, the United States is engaged in a war against terrorism. But this war has a unique twist for Americans. We are not fighting to stop a Hitler or godless Communism. In fact, both sides of the current war frequently invoke God's name. Osama bin Laden, just weeks after some of his operatives slammed the planes into the World Trade Center, the Pentagon, and a Pennsylvania field, said the following in a videotaped message: "There is America, hit by god in one of its softest spots. Its greatest buildings were destroyed, thank god for that. There is America, full of fear from its north to its south, from its west to its east. Thank god for that."[3]

In America we are calling bin Laden evil personified. We pray to God that he, and others like him, will be found and stopped. Yet, Osama is giving thanks to "god" for the obvious "blessings" of destroyed buildings, thousands of deaths, and widespread fear. Are we talking about the same "God"? Beyond Islam, are other religions simply different, but equally valid, paths to the same Supreme Being, whatever name someone happens to give him or her—or it?

There is no question more important than this.

As I have illustrated through my experiences after the Columbine school shootings and the 2001 inauguration, in America we seem to be embracing the idea that one religion is as legitimate as another. Tolerance of the sincerity of others has become our creed. Sadly, though, we can be both sincere and wrong. When we are, the consequences can be catastrophic.

As a pilot, I have experienced the sensation known as *vertigo*. Vertigo occurs when a person becomes temporarily disoriented say, in a cloudbank, when you cannot see up, down, left, or right—the cloud masks your visibility. Your senses tell you that you are headed in a different direction than you are actually going. A pilot who succumbs to vertigo can fly his aircraft nose first into the ground, taking his life and the lives of those with him, all the while sincerely believing that he is heading in the right direction. His only hope for survival—for life—is to rely on his aircraft instruments, the objective standards of measurement that accurately portray what is really happening. Relativity is not an option in the cockpit!

In relationship to God, it is not enough to go on what feels right or what we sincerely believe is true. To have life eternal, we must relate to God on His terms, not ours. He is, after all, God. So, the test of any faith's validity is whether it conforms to His standard. It is not enough to have a subjective belief that is based on one's experience only; every person's belief system must be scrutinized and tested objectively as well.

With this in view, does bowing down to Allah mean the same thing as worshiping the God of the Bible? What about adherents of the nearly ten thousand other religions? When they pray or call out to some higher essence or being, are they all seeking to make contact with the same divine person? Or are there other gods?

The Bible tells us that there are other gods. Do they really exist? Are they real? They certainly seem real to those who worship them. Even God Almighty Himself acknowledged this was the case in the first commandment: "You shall have no other gods before Me."[4] That is the key point: There are false gods of this world and then there is the one true God, who revealed Himself in the Person of Christ. The Bible says:

> The idols of the nations are silver and gold,
> The work of men's hands.
> They have mouths, but they do not speak;
> Eyes they have, but they do not see;
> They have ears, but they do not hear;
> Nor is there any breath in their mouths.
> Those who make them are like them;
> So is everyone who trusts in them.[5]

The preeminence of the Lord Jesus Christ is what the writer to the Hebrews was referring to when he wrote:

> In the past God spoke to our forefathers through the prophets at many times and in various ways, but in these last days he has spoken to us by his Son, whom he appointed heir of all things, and through whom he made the universe. The Son is the radiance of God's glory and the exact representation of his being, sustaining all things by his powerful word. After he had provided purification for sins, he sat down at the right hand of the Majesty in heaven.[6]

We in America are pretty confused. It seems that we do not want to grapple with a truth made very plain in Scripture: There is only one true God. He alone is supreme, unlike man-made gods that attract followers on earth. This is a point made by the Old Testament prophet Elijah when he challenged the false gods of his day.

In the ninth century B.C., a wicked king by the name of Ahab ruled Israel. The Bible says that Ahab "did evil in the sight of the LORD, more than all who were before him."[7] Elijah was not intimidated by Ahab, however, and declared to him: "You have forsaken the commandments of the LORD and have followed the Baals."[8]

He then called for a showdown between the God of Israel and Ahab's gods. As hundreds of idol-worshiping priests gathered on

Mount Carmel, Elijah squared off against them and issued this ultimatum: "How long will you waver between two opinions? If the LORD is God, follow him; but if Baal is God, follow him."

Then Elijah proposed a contest. He said to them,

> I am the only one of the LORD's prophets left, but Baal has four hundred and fifty prophets. Get two bulls for us. Let them choose one for themselves, and let them cut it into pieces and put it on the wood but not set fire to it. I will prepare the other bull and put it on the wood but not set fire to it. Then you call on the name of your god, and I will call on the name of the LORD. The god who answers by fire—he is God.

The prophets of Baal (their god) went first. The Bible says:

> They called on the name of Baal from morning till noon. "O Baal, answer us!" they shouted. But there was no response; no one answered. And they danced around the altar they had made.
>
> At noon Elijah began to taunt them. "Shout louder!" he said. "Surely he is a god! Perhaps he is deep in thought, or busy, or traveling. Maybe he is sleeping and must be awakened."
>
> So they shouted louder and slashed themselves with swords and spears, as was their custom, until their blood flowed. Midday passed, and they continued their frantic prophesying until the time for the evening sacrifice. But there was no response, no one answered, no one paid attention.
>
> Then Elijah said to all the people, "Come here to me." They came to him, and he repaired the altar of the LORD, which was in ruins. Elijah took twelve stones, one for each of the tribes descended from Jacob, to whom the word of the LORD had come, saying, "Your name shall be Israel." With the stones he built an altar in the name of the LORD, and he dug a trench around it large enough to hold two seahs [three gallons] of seed. He arranged the wood, cut the bull into pieces and laid it on the wood. Then he said to them, "Fill four large jars with water and pour it on the offering and on the wood."

> "Do it again," he said, and they did it again.
>
> "Do it a third time," he ordered, and they did it the third time. The water ran down around the altar and even filled the trench.
>
> At the time of sacrifice, the prophet Elijah stepped forward and prayed: "O LORD, God of Abraham, Isaac and Israel, let it be known today that you are God in Israel and that I am your servant and have done all these things at your command. Answer me, O LORD, answer me, so these people will know that you, O LORD, are God, and that you are turning their hearts back again.
>
> Then the fire of the LORD fell and burned up the sacrifice, the wood, the stones and the soil, and also licked up the water in the trench. When all the people saw this, they fell prostrate and cried, "The LORD—he is God! The LORD—he is God!"[9]

In the South where I live, an expression we use to affirm the obvious is, "I reckon!" When I read about the fire of God falling from heaven before the eyes of those idolaters gathered on Mount Carmel, "I reckon" they did throw themselves to the ground and cry out to the Lord!

Through the prophet Isaiah, God announced His supremacy in these words:

> "You are My witnesses," says the LORD,
> "And My servant whom I have chosen,
> That you may know and believe Me,
> And understand that I am He.
> Before Me there was no God formed,
> Nor shall there be after Me.
> I, even I, am the LORD,
> And besides Me there is no savior."[10]

My purpose in writing is not to provide a comparative religious textbook. However, with all of the confusion and controversy surrounding the various religions and the notion that every religion has a valid path to God, I think it is important to show how the Christian faith differs from other religions. In doing so, I do not write out of animosity toward those belief systems; I just want to show that there is a marked and drastic difference. Jesus Christ is the Name above all names, and He has been the most dominant influence on world history. And the evidence is so overwhelming. The reliability of Scripture, the evidence of the resurrection of Christ, and the common experiences of people worldwide whose lives have been radically changed all speak to the powerful differences between following Jesus Christ and any other "path to God." In fact, Jesus Himself spoke of the other paths when He said, "Enter by the narrow gate; for wide is the gate and broad is the way that leads to destruction, and there are many who go in by it. Because narrow is the gate and difficult is the way which leads to life, and there are few who find it."[11]

This truth is what motivates the ministry of Samaritan's Purse. Everything we do, we do in the Name of the Lord Jesus Christ. Our extensive relief work expands even into predominantly non-Christian countries. I have many friends who follow other religions, and the violent tactics of some of their fellow believers horrify them.

However, I will say pointedly that horrendous intolerance is practiced in some of those faiths. In some Hindu societies, for example, Christian churches are burned, and pastors and missionaries are killed because they testify to the one true God.

Islam—unlike Christianity—has among its basic teachings a deep intolerance for those who follow other faiths. Much is said and published today about how peace-oriented Islam is; however, a little scrutiny reveals quite the opposite. For example, the Hadith, the publication of the sayings of Muhammad and his early followers, states that the prophet Muhammad said, "One (military) raid for the cause of god is better than seventy hajj (pilgrimages to Mecca).[12]

That does not mean that all Muslims practice this doctrine or seek to harm those of other faiths. Certainly some followers of Islam are peaceloving. Let's not be naive. Islam is a proselytizing religion. Although Muslims profess that "there is no compulsion in religion," the Koran approves holy war (jihad) and high taxation against non-Muslims in order to make them submit to Islam.[13]

Sura 9:29 states: "Fight those who do not believe in Allah, nor in the latter day, nor do they prohibit what Allah and His Messenger have prohibited, nor follow the religion of truth, out of those who have been given the Book [people of the Book are the Jews and the Christians], until they pay the tax in acknowledgement of superiority and they are in a state of subjection."

During the early days of the war in Afghanistan, William F. Buckley wrote:

> We now have Islam to deal with. We do not need to make the point that its political and economic record is miserable; that only one of 18 Muslim states (Turkey) is democratically governed . . . It is thought to be a sign of toleration to defer to Islam as simply another religion. It isn't that . . . Carefully selected, there are Koranic preachments that are consistent with civilized life. But on September 11 we were looked in the face by a deed done by Muslims who understood themselves to be acting out Muslim ideals. It is all very well for individual Muslim spokesmen to assert the misjudgment of the terrorist, but the Islamic world is substantially made up of countries that ignore, or countenance, or support terrorist activity.[14]

When the last battle is fought and the smoke clears on this war against terrorism, the conflict between Islam and Christianity and the differences between the teaching of Muhammad and the teaching of Christ will still exist. What, then, are some of the key differences?

CHRISTIANITY AND ISLAM: THE DIFFERENCES

Although on the surface there may appear to be similarities between Christianity and Islam, these two are as different as lightness and darkness. Whole books have been written on this topic, but briefly stated, some of the critical differences include the following:

Christianity came into being when Jesus Christ—the sinless Son of God and Himself God—died to redeem a lost world back to God by giving Himself on the cross as a sacrifice for our sins. Islam, on the other hand, was founded by a mere human being, a warrior by the name of Muhammad, in whose teachings we see the tactic of "conversion by conquest," through violence if necessary.[15] Clearly, it appears that the ultimate objective of Islam is world domination.

Christianity has the Bible as its source of written truth; Islam has the Koran as its source.

The Bible (from a Greek word that means "books"), although written by at least thirty-five authors from a wide spectrum of backgrounds over a period of sixteen hundred years, is a book that has incredible unity in its message. The Bible has two major divisions: the Old and New Testaments. My friend and mentor, the late Roy Gustafson, a world-renowned authority on prophecy and the Bible lands, presented the divisions this way:

> The New Testament is *contained* in the Old Testament.
> The Old Testament is *explained* in the New Testament.
>
> The New Testament is *concealed* in the Old Testament.
> The Old Testament is *revealed* in the New Testament.
>
> The Old Testament *anticipates* the New Testament.
> The New Testament *authenticates* the Old Testament.
>
> In the Old Testament the New Testament *lies hidden.*
> In the New Testament the Old Testament *lies open.*
>
> The Old Testament *foreshadows* the New Testament.
> The New Testament *fulfills* the Old Testament.
>
> In the Old Testament they were always *seeking.*
> In the New Testament they *found.*
>
> The Old Testament *predicts* a Person.
> The New Testament *presents* that Person.
>
> And that Person is the Lord Jesus Christ—who fully validated the Old Testament.

The Pentateuch (the first five books of the Bible) *presents* the Figures of Christ.

The Psalms *present* the Feelings of Christ.
The Prophets *present* the Foretellings of Christ.

The Gospels *present* the Facts of Christ.
The Epistles *present* the Fruits of Christ.[16]

The Bible is the most widely read book in history and certainly the most influential. Critics have tried for centuries to discredit the Bible but have failed. The Bible is validated by outstanding original sources.

In contrast to the Bible, Islam's book, the Koran (a word meaning "recitation" in Arabic), was compiled over a period of twenty-three years during Muhammad's lifetime and is viewed by Muslims as taking precedence over the Bible. (The Koran is about four-fifths as long as the New Testament and divided into 114 chapters, called Suras.) The Koran contains the supposed revelations and visions of Muhammad as well as his teachings that were recorded by others. Included in the Koran are stories lifted and twisted from the Old and New Testaments. Over the years additional sayings of Muhammad and his early followers were compiled. These are called the Hadith. The Koran has not had the widespread effect on the Western and civilized cultures of the world that the Bible has had.

The number one difference between Islam and Christianity is that the god of Islam is not the God of the Christian faith. In the Christian faith, the God that is worshiped is the Almighty God, who has revealed himself in human form in the person of Jesus Christ, God's Son. The god of Islam is not a father and does not have a son, and to a Muslim, that very thought is blasphemous.[17]

The Bible teaches that individuals have a free will in making decisions about God; Islam often relies on force, intimidation, or conquering of entire nations to recruit converts.

Islam takes a hard-line approach to adherents of other faiths. A non-Muslim can easily become one, but if a Muslim decides to convert to Christianity or another religion, under Islamic law—if the individual does not recant—he risks almost certain death. Muslims are free to worship Allah, and even proselytize in the United States, but Christians are not free to worship the Son of God, the Lord Jesus Christ, or openly discuss their faith in most Muslim countries.

You may recall that in August of 2001, Dayna Curry and Heather Mercer, two female missionaries to Afghanistan, were imprisoned for months by the Taliban (which means "students of Islam"), for showing the Jesus Film on CD Rom in a private home. The film portrays the life of Christ. The young women eventually were freed only after the United States military drove the Taliban from power.

In countries like Sudan, when the government adopts Islamic law, that's it. There is no democracy, all laws are based on the Koran, and religious freedom is limited. That's why this war has raged for seventeen years. The Christians do not want to raise their children in Islamic schools. They want to be free to worship the Name. For those outside the Jewish and Christian faiths, such as Hindus, the Koran is even less tolerant, and idolaters are candidates for persecution and death. It says, "But when the forbidden months are past, then fight and slay the idolaters wherever ye find them, and take them, and prepare for them each ambush."[18]

The Christian message is God's love and forgiveness of our sins through faith in Jesus Christ—a gift that an individual is free to accept or reject. Although there have been disgusting acts done at times by wicked people claiming the name of Jesus, Christ Himself never advocated holy-war tactics, violence, misrepresentation, bribery, or coercion to make converts.

To many Muslims, young men and women who strap explosives to their bodies, walk into crowds as human bombs, and take the lives of innocent people are elevated and revered as martyrs. The hijackers used this same tactic on 9/11. They commandeered American airplanes, cut the throats of the pilots, slashed the passengers and crew, and then slammed the planes into New York skyscrapers. As President George W. Bush powerfully declared, "They are not martyrs, they are murderers." These "suicide bombers" have gained respect among Muslims due to the lack of condemnation by Muslim clerics. In fact many condone the practice. According to a *New York Times* article, Yasir Arafat's wife, Suha al-Taweel Arafat, told an Arabic language magazine that she endorsed suicide attacks as legitimate. She went on to say that if she had a son there would be no greater honor than to sacrifice him for the Palestinian cause.[19] In contrast, a Christian martyr is one who loses his or her life because of their faith.

In *Jesus Among Other Gods*, Ravi Zacharias wrote,

> The teaching of Jesus is clear. No one ought to be compelled to become a Christian. This sets the Christian faith drastically apart from Islam. In no country where the Christian faith is the faith of the majority is it illegal to propagate another faith. There is no country in the world that I know of where the renunciation of one's Christian faith puts one in danger of being hunted down by the powers of state. Yet, there are numerous Islamic countries where it is against the law to publicly proclaim the Gospel of Jesus Christ, and where a Muslim who renounces belief in Islam to believe in anything else risks death.[20]

I love what my dear friend Roy Gustafson often said: "Religion is what sinful people try to do for a Holy God, and the Gospel is the Good News of what a Holy God has already done for sinful people."[21]

Christianity views marriage as a relationship of equals with different roles; Islam essentially views marriage as a master-servant arrangement, with the husband possessing abusive power over his wife.

In view of the way women are degraded in many Islamic nations, it intrigues me that there is not more attention given this by Western media and women's rights advocacy groups. I remember the howling by some of these groups that went on when the Southern Baptist Convention issued a statement about the roles of men and women in marriage. While acknowledging the biblical teaching that men and women are of equal worth before God, they also recognized that God created men and women for unique functions and roles. This biblical teaching about women being submissive to their husbands had many media commentators foaming at the mouth with outrage.[22]

Yet until the war against terrorism began, very little was said about the shameful subjugation of women in Islamic countries such as Afghanistan, Saudi Arabia, and Iran—where the right of husbands to whip their wives was enforced by the government. In Saudi Arabia, women are not permitted to drive cars. In most Muslim countries, women have to have their heads and faces covered and generally are treated as second-class citizens. Furthermore, Muslims are allowed to practice polygamy, having up to four wives at any one time. If they decide they want another wife and already have four, they can divorce one and marry another. The woman who is divorced takes nothing out of the marriage; she cannot take the children and has no right to possessions, in most cases, she has no legal rights. She is simply discarded.

Jesus Christ is the One who elevated women and gave them a place of honor. Islam teaches not just that men and women have different functions and roles, but that men are actually superior to women. One Hadith goes so far as to say that a woman's intelligence and religion are deficient. Muhammad supposedly stated that the testimony of a woman is worth half the testimony of a man, because a woman's brain is deficient.[23]

Compare that with the encounter Jesus had with the woman in the book of Mark.[24] He dared to converse with someone that everyone else shunned due to her painful and chronic illness lasting twelve years; yet, Jesus stopped to heal her in the midst of a clamoring crowd. To a woman caught in adultery, He imparted forgiveness and the true love that her heart was craving.[25] To women who thought they had lost the One dearest to them, He gave the matchless privilege of being the first eyewitnesses of the resurrected Lord of lords.[26]

I like these conclusions from R. C. Sproul: "There are two other vital differences between Christianity and Islam. Islam has no Cross and no resurrection, articles of the faith that are of the essence of Christianity and of ultimate importance to the plan of the God of the Bible. Mohammed made no atonement for our sins when he died. And when he died, he remained so."[27]

In summary, the god of Islam is not the God of Christianity. The doctrines of Scripture are not the doctrines of the Koran.[28] Heaven for Christians[29] is not the same place as the paradise sought by Muslims.

For anyone to say that the two faiths worship the same God is incredibly uninformed. As someone so eloquently has said, "The god of Islam requires you to give your son to die for him. The God of the Bible gave His Son to die for you."

The current warfare is a classic struggle that will end with the second coming of Christ. Ultimately, the "war against terrorism" is just another conflict between evil and the Name.

OTHER RELIGIONS

Much has been said about Islam since 9/11. Maybe you are wondering if other religions have similar flaws. At the end of his life, it is quoted that Buddha apparently said he was still looking for truth. Christ, on the other hand, declared, "I am the . . . truth."[30]

Hinduism has over three hundred million gods. In teaching reincarnation, it consigns people to reap in the present lifetime the consequences of deeds in previous lifetimes.[31] The Christian faith teaches, "For by grace you have been saved through faith, and that not of yourselves; it is the gift of God, not of works, lest anyone should boast."[32]

God's Word clearly teaches that there is only one road to the one true God.

Detailed study of the roughly ten thousand religions in the world would expose a smorgasbord of beliefs almost impossible to categorize. When you boil it all down, though, it's very simple. The line of demarcation between the Christian faith and every other religion hinges on these truths:

- Jesus Christ is uniquely God.
- We are made right with God through faith in Christ alone, who once and for all shed His blood and died on the cross for our sins, then rose from the dead.
- The Holy Bible, God's Word, is the only infallible Book for faith and practice.

When measured against these standards, the religions of the world pale in comparison with the Name Jesus. You can accept Him or you can reject Him. The choice is yours. What will you do with the claims of Jesus Christ?

A THREAT TO THE GOSPEL

So why have I presented all this information? Because we need to know the truth about other religions: We are not worshiping the same God. Many people believe that there are many roads to God. Hindus believe that they have a road to God. Muslims believe that they have a road to God. But Jesus said, "I am the way, the truth, and the life. No one comes to the Father except through Me."[33]

While we must not forget that our responsibility as followers of the Lord Jesus Christ is to spread His Name to the ends of the earth, it is important to be mindful also that our greatest weapons are not defensive. There is no name like the Name of Jesus. That's because there is no other Person like Jesus, the very Son of God who, after dying on the cross for our sins, rose from the grave.

The sword of Islam will rust.
The flower of Buddhism will wither.
The temples of Hinduism will crumble.[34]

But the Name of the Lord Jesus Christ will reverberate eternally as the one true God.

Imagine walking down a road and coming to a fork, one leading to eternal life and the other leading to hell. The problem is, you don't know which one leads where. Then, you notice two men—one living, one dead. Which one would you ask for direction? The living man, of course.[35]

Believers in Jesus Christ follow the Living One. He is alive today. No other faith makes this claim. When we share the Name with others, we proclaim a risen Savior and a living Lord!

7

THE IMPORTANCE OF A NAME

Are you aware that your good name is worth a fortune?

The Bible substantiates this! The wisest man who ever lived, King Solomon, wrote: "A good name is more desirable than great riches; to be esteemed is better than silver or gold."[1] Solomon also said, "A good name is better than fine perfume."[2]

Why is a good name worth "millions"? It all traces back to God and the value He places on a name—His own and all others.

In the early pages of Scripture, we gather clues about the importance of the names of God. One of the first commands given to Adam was to name the animals.[3] When God created a helpmate for him, Adam named her Eve.[4] But where did Adam get *his* name?

It makes sense that God named Adam. But God gave him a name that reflects his origin . . . he came from the earth. Can you imagine? Adam rises from the dirt, inhales his first gasp of air, dusts himself off, looks around, then suddenly he hears a sound—the voice of his Maker speaking his name—"Adam." That gives me chills.

Because of my work with Samaritan's Purse, I have witnessed

some unusual events over the years that are not necessarily common to everyone's walk of life. During the war in Rwanda, when the Hutus killed an estimated two million Tutsis, we had a medical team working in the northern mountains among the Tutsi tribes. The United Nations abandoned them; the world watched in horror. Neither the United States nor any other nation came to their rescue. In spite of this horrific slaughter of innocent life, the Tutsis survived and eventually won the war.

An orphanage was given to Samaritan's Purse to manage and operate. I recall one day walking out behind the orphanage and noticing a scene I will never forget. Tutsis had been killed by the Hutus several weeks earlier, leaving behind no graves, no names, just decaying flesh from several dozen bodies where they fell. There were so many corpses throughout the country that it was impossible to bury them all.

After several months had passed, I returned once again to that very same spot in Rwanda. I looked around in amazement to see only traces of scattered bones; a tooth or a skull here and there was all that was left. The corpses had literally returned to the earth. I could not help but think that God knew each one who had been slaughtered by name; and they all had souls precious to Him.

In Old Testament times, each Hebrew name had a meaning and became an important part of a child's life. In ancient Jewish culture, a person's name was believed to significantly reveal his character and personality. So, for example, the name that the sly and shifty Jacob bore meant "heel grabber." How appropriate! To know Jacob's name was to truly understand something significant about him.[5]

There are many accounts in Scripture where God Himself gave men new names—sometimes at critical points in their lives. Abraham is the first example recorded. Until God made the covenant with Abraham, he was known as Abram or "exalted father." But following God's promise to Abram that he would have multitudes of descendants, God changed "Abram" to "Abraham," which means "father of many nations."[6]

It is fascinating to read the accounts of how God originally revealed the Name by which He wanted to be known. No wonder God calls each one by name.

BURN, BUSH, BURN

Recently I flew to Africa to see some of our relief work in progress and to visit our hospital in the southern Sudan, bombed seven times by the Sudanese government. When our work was complete, we returned to Naïrobi and then on to Rome where we were going to spend the night. Our plane refueled in Jeddah and we continued our flight toward Italy.

I have been flying for more than thirty years. Sitting in the nose of an airplane, a pilot can see vividly some of the most beautiful sunrises, sunsets, topography, that one can possibly imagine. On this particular spring day, the skies were crystal clear. Our flight path took us along the Red Sea to the very tip of the Sinai Peninsula. From there, our flight turned in a westerly direction over Cairo. At thirty-nine thousand feet, I could clearly see the Nile River, the longest river in the world, known as the "life of Egypt." It looked like a ribbon flowing out of the desert into the sea. Even at this altitude the Pyramids could be clearly seen.

As I looked out the right side of the cockpit, the Sinai Peninsula was still in view. I thought about Moses giving up his life as a prince to escape into the wilderness where he would meet God in an unusual way.

Let's go back some thirty-five hundred years to that riverbank of the Nile when the Jews were enslaved in Egypt. Pharaoh, the supreme ruler of the land in that day, was worried that the Hebrew population was growing too fast. He feared that maybe one day the Hebrews would outnumber the Egyptians. Pharaoh commanded that all infant Hebrew boys be killed. One Hebrew mother placed her son in a small basket in the reeds along the shore of the Nile, and the baby was later discovered by the daughter of Pharaoh. She took him as her own and named him Moses, meaning "taken out of the waters," and raised him in Pharaoh's court as a prince of Egypt. This prepared Moses for the task that God would call him to later in life. But it would not be revealed to him until he had cut all ties to Egypt. In his darkest hour while exiled in the Sinai Desert, God revealed Himself to Moses in a mysterious and miraculous way.

In the book of Exodus, we read the account where Moses heard from God's own lips His holy Name:

> Now Moses was tending the flock of Jethro his father-in-law, the priest of Midian. And he led the flock to the back of the desert, and came to Horeb, the mountain of God. And the Angel of the LORD appeared to him in a flame of fire from the midst of a bush. So he looked, and behold, the bush was burning with fire, but the bush was not consumed.
>
> Then Moses said, "I will now turn aside and see this great sight, why the bush does not burn."
>
> So when the LORD saw that he turned aside to look, God called to him [by name] from the midst of the bush and said, "Moses, Moses!" And he said, "Here I am."

Before we continue the story, I think it is important to point out that Moses was alert and obedient enough to notice that God was seeking to communicate with him and he was willing to listen. I wonder how many "burning bushes" in life you and I have missed because we were too focused on tending to our cares of the day.

Back to Exodus:

> Then He said, "Do not draw near this place. Take your sandals off your feet, for the place where you stand is holy ground." Moreover He said, "I am the God of your father—the God of Abraham, the God of Isaac, and the God of Jacob." And Moses hid his face, for he was afraid to look upon God.
>
> And the LORD said: "I have surely seen the oppression of My people who are in Egypt, and have heard their cry because of their taskmasters, for I know their sorrows. So I have come down to deliver them out of the hand of the Egyptians, and to bring them up from that land to a good and large land, to a land flowing with milk and honey

> . . . Now therefore, behold, the cry of the children of Israel has come to Me, and I have also seen the oppression with which the Egyptians oppress them. Come now, therefore, and I will send you to Pharaoh that you may bring My people, the children of Israel, out of Egypt."

One reason God chose Moses for this great leadership position was the fact that Moses had already made a choice. He had turned his back on the pleasures of Egypt, and the power of Pharaoh's house, to identify with his people and their suffering. He had the same kind of compassion for the Hebrews and their plight that God had.

The book of Hebrews elaborates: "By faith Moses, when he became of age, refused to be called the son of Pharaoh's daughter, choosing rather to suffer affliction with the people of God than to enjoy the passing pleasures of sin, esteeming the reproach of Christ greater riches than the treasures in Egypt; for he looked to the reward."[7]

Going on . . .

> But Moses said to God, "Who am I that I should go to Pharaoh, and that I should bring the children of Israel out of Egypt?"
>
> So He said, "I will certainly be with you. And this shall be a sign to you that I have sent you: When you have brought the people out of Egypt, you shall serve God on this mountain."

Some time later, it was on this very mountain that Moses met with God again and received the Ten Commandments.

> "Then Moses said to God, "Indeed, when I come to the children of Israel and say to them, 'The God of your fathers has sent me to you,' and they say to me, 'What is His name?' what shall I say to them?"
>
> And God said to Moses, "I AM WHO I AM." And He said, "Thus you shall say to the children of Israel, 'I AM has sent me to you.'"[8]

There it is: the first instance in the Bible where God literally tells a man what He is to be called. He does not come up with some grandiose, unique-sounding name! He just says, "Tell them I AM has sent you."

What kind of name is that for the Ruler of all? "I AM"? I am what? *I am God*. The actual word God used to describe Himself was "Yahweh" or "Jehovah," based on the verb "to be," which of course means simply "I AM who I am."

But with closer examination there is more to the meaning of "I AM" than first meets the eye. By calling Himself such a name, God was stating that He is and will always be the infinite and personal Lord of all who is behind everything and to whom everything ultimately is traced. His name, "I am who I am," shouts the truth that no one and nothing else can or will ever define God but God Himself.

God's name stems from the very essence of His rock-solid integrity and reputation. It is as if God said to Moses, "Oh, you want to know My name? I am not sure why you even needed to ask, but if you insist, it is I AM who I am! You can trust Me to be true to My Word because I am who I appear to be. There are no others like Me. My name is above reproach. When I promise something, consider it done."

His Name was too holy to use casually; Yahweh had commanded that His Name not be taken in vain. Out of fearful reverence, the Jews would not even speak the sacred name YHWH (pronounced "Yahweh"). They used other terms, such as "My Lord" (Adonai). When the vowels of Adonai accompanied YHWH, the word *Jehovah* resulted.[9]

Because I AM was so enormously encompassing, to adequately describe Him, a great host of names for God came into use by the children of Israel:

Jehovah-jireh	"The-Lord-Will-Provide"
Jehovah-nissi	"The-Lord-Is-My-Banner"
Jehovah-shalom	"The-Lord-Is-Peace"
Jehovah-shammah	"The-Lord-Is-There"
Jehovah-tsebaoth	"The-Lord-of-Hosts"
Jehovah Elohe Israel	"Lord-God-of-Israel"[10]

God reveres His Name highly. Every man, woman, boy, and girl is made in His image; it is important to Him that we treasure our own names and that we not take lightly the supreme value of a "good name."

THE SHEPHERD KNOWS HIS SHEEP

We read the words of our Lord Jesus with even greater excitement: "I am the good shepherd; and I know My sheep, and am known by My own."[11]

In a very real sense, the shepherd possesses his sheep. A shepherd in the rugged parts of Lebanon was once asked if he knew each one of his sheep. The shepherd replied, "If you blindfold me and bring me to any of my sheep, I can tell if it is mine by putting my hands on its face." The Lord Jesus felt this same close acquaintance with His followers when He said, "I know My sheep and am known of Mine."

The story is told of a pastor who was making a survey of the community around his parish. In his questioning he asked one woman, "How many children do you have?"

She started to name them: "Mary, John, Joseph, Anne . . ."

The pastor interrupted her and said, "I don't want the names, just the number!"

She then answered with a sense of righteous indignation, "Sir! My children do not have numbers, they have names!"

The Good Shepherd knows His sheep by name—every one of them.

"Adam, where are you?"

Hagar, on her way to Egypt, hears, "What ails you, Hagar?"

"Abraham, Abraham . . . Lay not your hand upon the lad."

"Elijah, what are you doing here?"

In the New Testament, the mere calling her by name made Mary recognize her risen Lord. "He calls His own sheep by name."[12]

BEARING A NAME WELL

Effort is required to keep a name good.

I have the privilege to bear my father's name, and I am blessed to this day to have a family name that is honored in my community and around the world. But I cannot, nor can you, ride on the success of someone else's name. However, in time, you will be remembered for your own name. Each one of us has the responsibility to guard and protect his own name.

There are those with names that at one time enjoyed a good reputation such as Congressman Gary Condit. Whether it is right or wrong, because of the attention the media have given the story, his once well-respected name now brings up connotations of political sleaze and mistrust.

When Enron, a great Texas-based energy giant and one of the leading companies in the world, is mentioned today, it brings up thoughts of greed, mismanagement, manipulation, shredding of documents and the like.

Osama bin Laden came from a well-respected family in Saudi Arabia known for success in construction. Now at the mention of his name, we think of terrorism, mass murder, and evil personified.

Then there are those who lived life in such a way that their names will go down in history with great integrity and respect. No matter how careful you are, sometimes circumstances and events out of your control can threaten the very integrity of a name.

Several centuries before Jesus Christ, Alexander the Great came out of Macedonia and Greece to conquer the Mediterranean world. He did not know it, but God was using him to prepare the way for the coming of the Messiah—for it was as a result of Alexander's conquests that Greek was established as the common language of the Grecian, and later even Roman, Empire.

On one of his campaigns, Alexander the Great received a message that one of his soldiers had displayed cowardice in the face of the enemy and was brought before Alexander. Standing there before this great dreaded warrior and conqueror of the known world, Alexander asked the young soldier, "What is your name?"

The reply came back with fear and trembling, "Sir, my name is Alexander." To this, the great commander bristled and shouted to the young soldier, "Change your behavior or change your name."

This story has a lesson. When people call themselves Christians they are identifying with Jesus Christ. When they wear crosses, or put

Christian stickers on their cars, they are being witnesses for Him and are identified with the Name.[13]

It reminds me of my brother-in-law after my sister put a bumper sticker on the back of his car: "Honk if you love Jesus." He was a tough guy, a former football player and weight lifter. People would drive by and honk their horn at him. He would get mad, roll down the window and shake his fist and yell . . . hardly an example of Christ. He didn't know the sticker was there.

Old cowboys used to identify which ranch they worked for by saying: "I ride for the brand." They were identifying with the brand on the cattle.

If you wear signs of the Christian faith, be loyal to His cause, His teachings, and His commands.

OUR NAME QUESTIONED

The first week that President George W. Bush was in office, he announced the Faith-Based Initiative Plan, a program that gives government aid to religious groups performing certain services to people in local communities. Many liberal groups in the United States viewed this idea with great suspicion. There is an enormous paranoia about any potential blurring of the separation of church and state. The handwringers among us have deep anxieties that innocent people will be forced against their will to embrace "harmful religious ideas." So the idea that any faith group could receive government funds—no matter how valuable their contribution to the public good—is an abomination in their minds.

Samaritan's Purse became a target perhaps because I had prayed at the inauguration. Critics may have assumed that because I was seen with the president that somehow our ministry would be at the front of the line to receive faith-based initiative funding. That was not true. In fact, the Faith-Based Initiative Plan is basically for inner-city and domestic ministries. The majority of work that Samaritan's Purse does is overseas. From time to time, however, we have received a minimal amount of aid from federal agencies such as the United States Agency for International Development (USAID) and even the United Nations.

In the winter of 2001, Samaritan's Purse responded to needs in the aftermath of the massive earthquakes that destroyed much of rural El Salvador. Hundreds of thousands of people were homeless. Aftershocks still rumbled, causing more devastation and fear.

On March 5, the *New York Times* published an article accusing Samaritan's Purse of using government funds from USAID to assist in spreading the Gospel. Supposedly, we were forcing people to pray. Naturally, my name was brought up because I serve as the president of the organization. In the following days a media flurry of headlines read, "Feds Probe Graham's Ministry"; "Agency to Watch Ministry Accused of Mixing Religion with Earthquake Relief"; and "Graham Denies Using Tax Money to Proselytize."[14]

The media is very quick to pounce on a person's name and integrity when it suits their agenda. In this case, I don't believe their agenda was necessarily about me, or our work, but to cast a doubtful shadow on the president's Faith-Based Initiative. I suspect they were wanting to discredit him.

It is true that we had a volunteer in El Salvador who led in prayer before distributing some of our relief supplies. This is not uncommon. We do this quite often. We are a Christian evangelism relief-and-development organization. In this situation, however, USAID funds were not involved. In fact, USAID had not given us any money for our work in El Salvador at that time.

So what was the issue? I have no problem using government money to help people, as long as we do not compromise our message. When it comes to relief work, USAID states that we cannot use its funding for religious activities. That's fair, and I completely agree 100 percent. We have always abided by their restrictions in using such funds to build needed shelters and provide for physical needs. God has always provided, through His people, the funding needed to do His work. We have every right to pray with whomever we chose, and the right is ours to preach the Gospel as long as we do not use government funding for that purpose. Furthermore, we never force anyone to pray or take part in any ministry outreach in order for those in need to qualify for our assistance. We would never discriminate. If someone asked me to separate my work from my faith in order to receive funding from a government agency or foundation, I would refuse.

The reporter who went after this story was apparently eager to discredit the president, and he failed to look at all the facts. USAID had no choice but to investigate the situation after this report was released. However, after looking at all the facts, it was not long before USAID announced that Samaritan's Purse was in compliance and had not violated any of their policies. I am grateful that they worked quickly to resolve this issue so that it would not hamper our ongoing relief work and the people who were suffering in El Salvador.

A news release went out saying, "USAID and Samaritan's Purse have a significant and productive history of working together in addressing humanitarian and emergency relief needs in developing countries, USAID is confident that Samaritan's Purse is fully competent and able to fulfill all requirements for use of federal funds as a non-governmental organization (NGO) registered with USAID."[15]

When the facts were fully examined, to my knowledge the *New York Times* never printed another story or retraction, but it really doesn't matter. I don't have to worry about setting the record straight. People will say and think what they want, regardless of the truth.

When it comes to integrity, His Name stands the test of time—day in and day out. There is no greater challenge than to fix our eyes on Christ and live a life above reproach—keeping our words and actions above board—nothing hidden. God does not write anonymous letters; God puts His Name on everything that He does and says.

8

THE NAME IN TIME

The mountains of western North Carolina have always been my home. There were brief periods where I moved away to school and later for temporary work assignments, but the mountains have always drawn me back.

Autumn is one of my favorite times of year. I love hunting season—a chance to go into the woods on cool evenings, wake up in the early morning frost and smell the wet leaves . . . there is just something about fall that I love. Maybe it's the anticipation of knowing that Christmas is coming.

In the Graham home Christmas has always been fun. When I was small I recall my mother decorating the house, but she also encouraged us to look for opportunities to help others who had less than we did. Today Jane and I do the same, teaching our children to reach out to others in need so they can understand the meaning of Christmas. Unfortunately, today the real meaning gets lost in the material exploitation of our Lord's birth.

For the baby born in Bethlehem, the first Christmas was not about parties, wrapping paper, and "chestnuts roasting on an open fire." As C. S. Lewis said, "The Son of God became a man to enable men to become sons of God."[1]

EARLY VISITS

Many assume that the first appearance of Jesus occurred in Bethlehem—we even fix our calendar as B.C. or A.D.—before or after Christ's birth. But because Jesus is God, He has always existed. From the beginning of time He reigned from His throne in heaven. The book of John states, "In the beginning was the Word [Jesus], and the Word was with God, and the Word was God. He was in the beginning with God. All things were made through Him, and without Him nothing was made that was made."[2]

Many do not realize that long before Jesus arrived in Bethlehem, as a baby born to a virgin, there were numerous encounters with the Lord. This was the Son of God in pre-incarnate form. When the Word became flesh, the Bible says that He died on a Roman cross; He was buried and then rose again on the third day, according to the Scriptures. This happened on a hill called Mount Calvary.

In fact, it was on this very mountain ridge where, centuries before Jesus' death, that one of the most amazing incidents depicting the Cross of Christ occurred.

In Genesis we find the story of Abraham—the man with whom God made a covenant that promised he would be the father of many nations with descendants as numerous as the stars.[3] This promise puzzled Abraham and his wife, Sarah, because they were now elderly and childless. But miraculously, God intervened and Sarah gave birth to a son, Isaac. Can you imagine Sarah's joy and thrill in her nineties to finally hold her own child? The promise had been fulfilled.

Then came perhaps the greatest test of faith and obedience a human father could ever face: "Now it came to pass after these things that God tested Abraham, and said to him, 'Abraham!' And he said, 'Here I am.'"

When God calls us in life we need to respond. And Abraham's response was, "Here I am." Here I am to do Thy will. Here I am to go where You want me to go, here I am to say what You want me to say, here I am to lay down my life. I am here to do Your pleasure. This needs to be the response of every follower of the Lord Jesus Christ."

"Then He said, 'Take now your son, your only son Isaac, whom you love, and go to the land of Moriah, and offer him there as a burnt offering on one of the mountains of which I shall tell you.'"

Can you imagine? I am a father of four children. If God asked me to take any one of them and do this . . . I cannot fathom the thought, but Abraham said, "Here I am."

"So Abraham rose early in the morning and saddled his donkey, and took two of his young men with him, and Isaac his son; and he split the wood for the burnt offering, and arose and went to the place of which God had told him. Then on the third day Abraham lifted his eyes and saw the place afar off."

Now a picture is beginning to unfold. A parallel. God gave His Son, His only Son, to die for the sins of this world, and on the third day He rose from the grave. Abraham was asked to take his son, his only son, and offer him as a sacrifice to God. Abraham obeyed, and on the third day of the journey he looked and saw in the distance the place where he was to sacrifice his son.

"And Abraham said to his young men, 'Stay here with the donkey; the lad and I will go yonder and worship, and we will come back to you.'"

Now we get a glimpse. Abraham knows that somehow God will provide for him, because he says to the young men, "I will go yonder and worship, and *we* will come back to you."

"So Abraham took the wood of the burnt offering and laid it on Isaac his son; and he took the fire in his hand, and a knife, and the two of them went together." Remember, the Lord Jesus Christ carried the wood of the cross upon His shoulders, and here we see that the wood was placed upon Isaac.

> But Isaac spoke to Abraham his father and said, "My father!" And he said, "Here I am, my son." Then he said, "Look, the fire and the wood, but where is the lamb for a burnt offering?"

> And Abraham said, "My son, God will provide for Himself the lamb for a burnt offering." So the two of them went together.

It is important to look at this revelation: God would one day provide for Himself "the" Lamb. Isaac was not the Lamb—it would be the very Son of God.

"Then they came to the place of which God had told him. And Abraham built an altar there and placed the wood in order; and he bound Isaac his son and laid him on the altar, upon the wood." Bible scholars estimate that Isaac was probably close to twenty years of age. It is interesting to note that there is no mention of Isaac resisting, and he was certainly strong enough as a young man to have fought his aged father. This is a picture of Christ; for when He went to the cross, He did not resist His Father in heaven but gave Himself willingly and submitted to His Father.

"And Abraham stretched out his hand and took the knife to slay his son. But the Angel of the LORD called to him from heaven and said, 'Abraham, Abraham!' So he said, 'Here I am.'" Here is Abraham again answering the call of the Lord. Here I am, Lord, to do Your will, to do Your pleasure.

> And He said, "Do not lay your hand on the lad, or do anything to him; for now I know that you fear God, since you have not withheld your son, your only son, from Me." Then Abraham lifted his eyes and looked, and there behind him was a ram caught in a thicket by its horns. So Abraham went and took the ram, and offered it up for a burnt offering instead of his son.

Remember, Isaac asked his father where the lamb was for the burnt offering. Abraham told him that God would provide for Himself a lamb. A ram is not a lamb. So this promise was not fulfilled at this time. However, the ram satisfied the sacrifice for the moment; for the Lamb that Abraham spoke of would not come for another two thousand years.

"And Abraham called the name of the place, The-LORD-Will-Provide;

as it is said to this day, 'In the mount of the LORD it shall be provided.'"[4] Two thousand years later, just a few miles from that very place, God Almighty provided that Lamb, His very own Son, the Lord Jesus Christ. Out of obedience to His Father, Jesus went to the cross. He was nailed to a tree. He was the sacrifice for our sins past, for our sins present, for the sins we will commit in the future. The shedding of His blood paid our debt of sin once and for all. Never again will there be the need for a sacrifice for sin. Never again will Jesus Christ have to die. Never again will an altar have to be built and a life be lost to satisfy God. The debt has been paid in full, and God confirmed it by raising Him from the dead.

A SMALL TOWN IN JUDEA

When the Lord Jesus Christ was born in Bethlehem, Judea was not of much importance to the superpowers of the ancient world. This small piece of real estate, under subjugation to Rome since 63 B.C., measured only about fifty-six miles from north to south and east to west.[5] Except for brief bursts of independence, the Jews living in Judea had been under the thumb of other nations for centuries. The glory days of Israel under King David were a distant memory.

The town of Bethlehem was best known for its association with the revered King David, thus its title—"city of David." Bethlehem was the spot where Samuel had anointed David as king after God's rejection of King Saul for his disobedience. The prophet Micah predicted that Bethlehem would be the birthplace of a messiah or "anointed one" who would rescue His people.[6]

The Jews enjoyed some measure of self-governance and important freedoms even under Roman rule. They could conduct their work; for example, shepherds could tend their flocks on nearby hills without interference. The Jews were able to observe their religious practices, build synagogues, and maintain the temple in Jerusalem. Young Jewish men were not drafted into the Roman military.

Israel was under occupation by the most powerful military force ever up to that time. Military tactics of the Roman Legion have influenced the thinking of the greatest generals in history and are still taught in military schools and academies around the world. On numerous occasions, Hollywood has made films that depict the power of the Roman army during this time.

Jewish citizens learned to live under Roman occupation. But there was a minority of fanatic dissidents—the zealots—who sought to overthrow Roman rule because they thought it treason against God to pay tribute to the Roman emperor, since God alone was Israel's King.[7] Thus the real rub between the Jews and Romans came over their different understanding of God. The Romans celebrated tolerance much as America does today, eagerly assimilating the religions of conquered territories and welcoming many pagan gods. The Romans even granted deity status to some of their rulers, including Augustus, who was emperor during this time.[8]

The Jews of the first century were looking forward to the day when a "king of the Jews"—a mighty savior—would restore the kingdom of Israel and drive out occupying armies.

Before the arrival of the Lord Jesus Christ, there were many descriptions and names given to the coming Messiah: Immanuel (which means God with us), Wonderful Counselor, Mighty God, Everlasting Father, Prince of Peace, Great Light, Righteous King, Divine Servant, Elect One, Delight of God's Soul, Law-giver, Liberator, Arm of the Lord, Burden-bearer, Suffering Savior, Sin-bearer, Intercessor, Anointed Preacher, and Mighty Savior.[9] Again, we see the significance of a name.

No wonder the Jews looked for the One who would come to rescue them!

WELCOMING THE NAME-BEARER

We are familiar with the story of a carpenter named Joseph who was engaged to a young virgin named Mary. Perhaps we tend to skip by a bit too quickly the remarkable moment when God shared with a common Jewish maiden that she would give birth to the Promised One of Israel. She was the first to know the name He would bear.

The angel Gabriel visited Mary in the lower Galilean town of Nazareth, situated about ninety miles north of Bethlehem. Nazareth, which sat in a high valley twelve hundred feet above sea level, overlooked the main highway linking Damascus to the Mediterranean coast and Egypt. This was not a "backwoods" village, but a place where the latest news of the day was easily obtained.[10]

Mary, a virgin, had been promised in marriage to Joseph. Through the Holy Spirit, God formed and planted in her womb the life of His Son. When Joseph discovered that Mary, to whom he was engaged, was with child, he, being a righteous man, decided to end the relationship privately so as not to embarrass her and put her to public scorn. In the middle of the night, an angel of the Lord, Gabriel, appeared to Joseph and said: "Joseph, son of David, do not be afraid to take to you Mary your wife, for that which is conceived in her is of the Holy Spirit. And she will bring forth a Son, and you shall call His name JESUS, for He will save His people from their sins."[11]

Sometime after Gabriel's visit, Mary went to see her cousin Elizabeth, who miraculously, given her advanced age, was expecting a son; his name would be called John. Amazingly, when Mary entered Elizabeth's house, Elizabeth's baby "leaped" in her womb.[12] Can you imagine! The very baby who would become known as John the Baptist, yet unborn, recognized and acknowledged the presence of the greatest Name in heaven and on earth.

It was as if John's tiny body exclaimed, "Yes! Praise God He's here! I can't wait to get out into the world! Someday I'll be baptizing in the Jordan River and He will come to me. I can't wait to prepare the way for the Redeemer."

John was born for one purpose only: to prepare the way for the Lord.[13] Even before his birth, it seemed that John was beginning his mission!

The story of what happened later to John helps us understand clearly what it can mean to represent Jesus Christ. When you become a follower of His, you should give up your rights to have life unfold as you might want. After that dramatic day when John baptized Jesus, his ministry began to decline. Before Jesus' public ministry started, John drew multitudes as he preached. But when Jesus began to preach in the same areas and perform spectacular miracles, the crowds no longer flocked after John.

John knew his role and obeyed God by sticking to it. When some of his followers complained that Jesus was taking over the spotlight, John praised Jesus and simply said, "He must increase, but I must decrease."[14]

Circumstances worsened for John. He was thrown into prison for criticizing the immorality of the Jewish ruler Herod. Life in prison was difficult for John—locked in a dark, damp dungeon, deprived of food I suspect, and tortured endlessly. As time passed, John seemed to have some doubts about whether Jesus really was the Lamb of God. Just how accurate were the reports he was hearing about Jesus? There was no cable news to observe events as they unfolded.

John sent two of his followers to ask Jesus firsthand, "Are You really the One I thought You were?" Jesus told them to go back and tell John: "The blind see and the lame walk; the lepers are cleansed and the deaf hear; the dead are raised up and the poor have the Gospel preached to them."[15] And then Jesus said of John, "Among those born of women there has not risen one greater than John the Baptist; but he who is least in the kingdom of heaven is greater than he."[16]

I believe that when John's friends returned to John with this report, there was a loud "Amen! Praise God! Hallelujah!" that echoed through his prison cell. Later, John would pay the ultimate price for his faithfulness to God's Word when Herod had him beheaded to please his wicked wife.[17]

John the Baptist confronted sin and spoke the truth, and it cost him his very life. The purpose of life for John the Baptist was to prepare the way of the Lord.

Remember the brave martyr at Columbine High School, Cassie Bernall? Is it possible that her purpose in life was to make that statement, "Yes, I believe in God!"—words that would echo through hearts and even through school halls across this nation and around the world? In death Cassie's voice will be heard for generations. In the instant after the bullets ended her life on earth, I believe that she heard a beautiful voice say the most precious words of all, "Well done, My good and faithful servant." And when the executioner's ax fell on the neck of John the Baptist, I believe that he heard those same precious words: "Well done, My good and faithful servant."

RECEIVING HIS NAME

The One to save His people from their sins was born into the home of a carpenter. Joseph's greatest "claim to fame" to that point was his membership in Israel's premier bloodline—he was a descendant of the House of David. Isn't it of great interest that God would place His Son, who created the universe and all things, in the home of a carpenter, a builder? And later in life, when He began his ministry, He empowered His disciples spiritually—a task that He does even to this day to build His church.

The King of Glory could have chosen to be born into the family of a scientist, physician, or political leader. Or what about being the firstborn son of the chief rabbi—wouldn't that have been fitting? But Jesus came humbly to experience human life on earth so that He could relate to our sorrows and joys, and to live out His life in obedience to the Father's command.

Everything from Christ's miraculous birth to His resurrection was extraordinary. Jesus, our Savior, was given a holy name, a magnificent name, chosen by His heavenly Father and proclaimed by the angel Gabriel. As with everything else about this birth, the name, too, was perfect. Saving others was precisely the destiny for the Holy One of God taking shape in Mary's womb.

Although the story of the first Christmas is so familiar to us, we can only grasp a glimpse of what that night was really like. I am especially interested in the thoughts and feelings of this special couple, holding in their arms the Child who would forever change our world for good. The Name had come. I would guess at some moment, perhaps with knowing smiles, Mary and Joseph looked at one another and said reverently, "His Name is Jesus."

9

THE ADVANCE

It is the most fascinating fact of all time—how the Name of Jesus Christ spread around the world from the Judean town of Bethlehem. Think of it: He has transcended borders, and His love has broken barriers of race, culture, and language. His Name has dominated every century and has changed the course of history.

Think of what Christ did: He left his heavenly home, in obedience to His Father, came to this earth to live and to be one of us. Remember, this was God in human form—Immanuel—God with us. His motives would be misunderstood. Jesus willingly suffered in order to identify with us. His whole purpose and reason for coming was to give everything for us—including His precious blood and life.

Such is the story of those who generation after generation faithfully advanced the Name of Jesus, starting with the Great Commission given to the disciples, who were in many ways the first in a long line of missionaries.

What is required to represent the Name of the Lord Jesus? Total commitment, unwavering obedience, and personal sacrifice—being completely sold out to His cause.

Those words certainly describe the Lord Jesus and His ministry. He knew the world was hostile territory for those who love and obey God. The Devil, through his agents, sought to harm Jesus from the moment He came to earth. Herod, Rome's puppet ruler of Judea, tried to eliminate any competition to his kingdom with the slaughter of all the baby boys in Bethlehem. If Joseph had not listened to what the angel of the Lord had told him in a dream and escaped with Mary and Jesus to Egypt, what would have happened to the Lamb of God?

We know little about the thirty years of Jesus' life that preceded His baptism by John. From the beginning of His public ministry, nearly everything He did and said provoked controversy and conflict with religious leaders and some of His own earthly family—even His first miracle, changing water to wine at Cana, was controversial.

> There was a wedding in Cana of Galilee, and the mother of Jesus was there. Now both Jesus and his disciples were invited to the wedding. And when they ran out of wine, the mother of Jesus said to Him, "They have no wine." Jesus said to her, "Woman, what does your concern have to do with me? My hour has not yet come."[1]

Dr. J. Vernon McGee, one of the great Bible teachers of the twentieth century, makes some interesting points in his study *Thru the Bible*:

> When the angel Gabriel appeared to her [Mary] and told her that she was the one who was to bring forth the Messiah, Mary raised the question about the Virgin Birth, ". . . How shall this be, seeing I know not a man?" (Luke 1:34). Gabriel made it very clear that the Holy Spirit would come upon her and that which was conceived in her was holy. She showed her faith and submission when she said, ". . . Behold the handmaid of the Lord . . ." (Luke 1:38). From that moment, and during the intervening years, there was always a question about her virginity. People actually raised questions about

> Jesus. She is really saying, "Here is Your opportunity to perform a miracle and demonstrate that I am accurate when I said that You were virgin born and that You are the One whom I have claimed You are." . . . Here she is asking Him to do something that will demonstrate who He is to clear her name. He tells her that He is going to do just that—He will clear her name—but that the hour has not yet come.[2]

Three years later while hanging on the cross, Jesus said to His mother: "Behold thy son." Now His hour had come. His work was done. The task of redeeming sinful man to a Holy God was done and now her name could be cleared. As Dr. McGee says, "His [Jesus'] resurrection proves who He is."

In spite of controversy and opposition, Jesus accomplished in just three short years everything the Father had sent Him to do. The scope of His ministry was limited to a small area of approximately ten thousand square miles, about the equivalent of a small state.[3] The task of carrying the Good News of the Name to the rest of the world would be left to His followers. He warned them that doing so in His Name would bring opposition, resentment, and even death. Once Jesus said to His disciples, "If they persecuted Me, they will also persecute you . . . All these things they will do to you for My name's sake, because they do not know Him who sent Me."[4]

Jesus also gave an incredible promise, an opportunity to gain access and favor from God Almighty because of the Name: "Most assuredly, I say to you, whatever you ask the Father in My name He will give you."[5]

Those words were true when Jesus said them two thousand years ago, are true today, and will be true tomorrow and forever.

In this chapter, I want to give an abbreviated version of how this most powerful Name has advanced from a small town in Judea literally to the ends of the earth.[6] In no way is this a comprehensive list, but it contains snapshots of some of the great individuals who have been responsible for the advancement of the Name of the Lord Jesus Christ. We will see how God used them and how He might use you.

All are representative of millions who have obediently given their lives to the service of the King.

PAUL

No doubt, the greatest missionary of all time was the man named Saul (later Paul) who started his career as a persecutor of the church. Saul was a premier Pharisee who once made it a personal vendetta to oppose the blasphemous sect and hunt down Christians, throw them in prison, and—ideally—seek their execution. The Bible indicates that Saul consented to the stoning of Stephen, the first Christian martyr, and guarded the clothes of those killing him.[7] While on a trip to persecute and capture Christians in Damascus, Saul was surrounded by a light from heaven. He fell to his knees and the Lord Jesus said to him, "Saul, Saul, why are you persecuting Me?" In just seconds, the biggest opponent of the early church was blind, meek, and docile: "Lord, what do You want me to do?"[8] Ultimately, the Lord told Saul that he was a chosen vessel and would "bear [Christ's] name before Gentiles, kings, and the children of Israel." He also told him how much he would suffer for "My name's sake."[9]

Only days later, Paul the ex-Pharisee was back in the synagogues preaching that Christ was the Son of God. This was the beginning of Paul's missionary ministry. He would lead the early advance of the Name while completing four dangerous missionary journeys.

I like to think of Paul as the disciple who really replaced Judas, the disciple who betrayed Jesus and later hanged himself. I know that the other disciples cast lots and picked a man named Matthias to take that role. But we read nothing more about Matthias after this. But the Lord Jesus—just as He had with the original twelve disciples—called Paul on the road to Damascus.

Paul was a brave and passionate witness for the Gospel. He once summarized the price he had paid in representing Christ:

> I am more: in labors more abundant, in stripes above measure, in prisons more frequently, in deaths often. From the Jews five times I

> received forty stripes minus one. Three times I was beaten with rods; once I was stoned; three times I was shipwrecked; a night and a day I have been in the deep; in journeys often, in perils of waters, in perils of robbers, in perils of my own countrymen, in perils of the Gentiles, in perils in the city, in perils in the wilderness, in perils in the sea, in perils among false brethren; in weariness and toil, in sleeplessness often, in hunger and thirst, in fastings often, in cold and nakedness—besides the other things, what comes upon me daily: my deep concern for all the churches.[10]

Paul often found himself in trouble and ultimately ended up in prison where he represented the Name of Christ boldly to his cellmates and captors. He loved those he had ministered to and poured out his heart, wisdom, and advice in letters he wrote to the churches. Like his Master, Paul ended his earthly life with the shedding of his blood. Tradition has it that Paul was beheaded for his faith during the vicious persecution of Christians carried out by the Roman emperor Nero.[11]

Every Christian who will ever live owes a huge debt to this bold and brave missionary of the Gospel. God used Paul's sophisticated understanding of Scripture, his brilliance, and his passionate love for the Lord Jesus to articulate in writing so much of what we need to understand about God and His ways.

GEORGE WISHART

Let's jump ahead in history many centuries to tell the story of the Scottish martyr George Wishart, let me fill in a few blanks.

Since the church was born during the Roman rule, it was inevitable that the spread of the Gospel would be hindered or assisted by this superpower. Almost from the beginning, the Romans considered the Christian Church a problem and ended up persecuting Christians for 250 years. During this period, there were many martyrs for the faith, and the church actually grew in strength and numbers. Then in a 180-degree turnaround of the official position, the Roman emperor Constantine gave Christians freedom of worship in A.D. 313.

About eighty years later, Christianity became the official religion of the Roman Empire.

This turn of events was a mixed blessing. The movement of Christians from an outcast minority to part of the official status quo caused many to lose their spiritual edge. Some believers saw the need to pull away to maintain their fire. This happened within the church, such as during the Reformation when "protestors" pulled away from the Roman Catholic Church to become Protestants. Later in church history, believers became disgusted with the political shenanigans and pollution of faith that resulted when Christianity became the official state religion.

George Wishart was a missionary in his own country. He, like many others in history, represented the truth of Scripture and the pure Christian faith to those of his own generation. I already have mentioned my family roots in Scotland, so I am proud of my ancestors in that land who refused to recognize the King of England as the head of the church. They would only bow to Jesus Christ as their head, and for that many were persecuted.

Although Wishart is not one of my relatives, his story is a favorite because he stood so boldly and bravely for the truth. George was a teacher at the University of Cambridge who had beliefs offensive to the official church. For his refusal to recant, Wishart was arrested in 1543 and imprisoned in chains under charges of heresy. He was so effective in defending himself that those in authority worried that, if given enough opportunity to speak, he would win many people to his viewpoint.

He did have a way of getting under the skin of the religious authorities. Once he said to his accusers, "Your doctrine is full of blasphemous and abominable words coming from the devil. You should know my doctrine so I don't die unjustly to the peril of your own souls."[12]

Wishart was sentenced to hang. Among his last words to his supporters before he was led to the gallows were, "I do not fear this grim fire. If any persecution comes to you for the Word's sake, do not fear those who kill the body but cannot kill the soul. Tonight I will dine with the Lord."

Following the example of the Lord Jesus on the cross, Wishart then asked God to forgive those who had condemned him. Amazingly, the hangman then kneeled before him and asked that George forgive him for participating in the execution. Wishart asked the hangman to come near and kissed him on the cheek. "There's a token of my forgiveness," George told him. "Do your job."

The man did his duty, and George Wishart stepped into eternity to have that meal with the Lord Jesus.

On every continent, graves dot the landscape where martyrs paid with their blood to advance the Gospel. All who profess allegiance to Christ must be ready at a moment's notice to do the same thing, to have conviction like the Apostle Paul, who said, "For I am ready not only to be bound, but also to die at Jerusalem for the name of the Lord Jesus."[13] The last book of the Bible, the revelation of the Lord Jesus Christ recorded by the Apostle John, makes clear that such sacrifice does not escape notice in heaven:

> When He [Jesus] opened the fifth seal, I saw under the altar the souls of those who had been slain for the word of God and for the testimony which they held.
>
> And they cried with a loud voice, saying, "How long, O Lord, holy and true, until You judge and avenge our blood on those who dwell on the earth?"
>
> Then a white robe was given to each of them; and it was said to them that they should rest a little while longer, until both the number of their fellow servants and their brethren, who would be killed as they were, was completed.[14]

I do not know about you, but reading that gives me goose bumps—these brave followers of the Lord Jesus are so precious to God that their numbers have been predetermined. Later in the Revelation, we read that those who were "beheaded for their witness to Jesus and for the word of God" will later live and reign "with Christ for a thousand years."[15]

None of us want to lose life "prematurely," but losing life for the cause of Christ is not really losing. Jesus said, "He who finds his life will lose it, and he who loses his life for My sake will find it."[16]

Jim Elliott, one of the great missionaries of the last century to Ecuador, who was martyred for his faith, wrote in his journal: "He is no fool who gives what he cannot keep to gain what he cannot lose."[17]

WILLIAM CAREY

In the late 1700s, a great burst of missionary fervor began in the United Kingdom. A man who was a cobbler by trade, William Carey, emerged as the leader of this movement to spread the Good News of Jesus Christ.

When Carey was a young man and an apprentice learning the shoemaker's trade, a coworker named John Warr faithfully and insistently shared the Gospel with him. William resisted the wooing and conviction of the Holy Spirit, but eventually his heart softened, and he came to Christ. He devoted himself to Scripture study, and while still working as a cobbler, pastored a small church. Above all, he loved to share the Gospel and see people come to Christ.

It may surprise us now, but during Carey's day, at least in protestant circles, the idea of sending missionaries to foreign lands was not widely supported. Carey could not understand this attitude because God had burned the words of Isaiah 54:5 into his soul: "He is called the God of the whole earth."

One day at a meeting of pastors, William was proposing that the Great Commission given to the apostles should be a mandate for every generation. One of the men listening interrupted Carey, "Sit down, young man, sit down and be still. When God wants to convert the heathen, He will do it without consulting either you or me."[18]

Carey respectfully backed off at the meeting, but his desire to reach the lost in "heathen nations" never died. For eight years he studied the unreached nations of the world and as a result issued a pamphlet entitled "The Enquiry." He wrote, "Surely it is worthwhile to lay ourselves out with all our might in promoting Christ's Kingdom!"

In a fiery sermon, Carey issued a ringing challenge that still motivates Christians today: "Expect great things from God. Attempt great things for God." His holy enthusiasm stirred the pastors to start a "Baptist

Society for propagating the Gospel among the heathen." This was the beginning of the modern mission movement as we know it today.

It was not enough for William Carey, though, to just talk about advancing the Gospel. God actually called him to go to India. When William and his family arrived in Calcutta in 1793, he witnessed a desperate spiritual plight of the Indian people. They showed enormous devotion to pagan gods. Devotees to these religions lay on beds of spikes, gazed at the sun until they went blind, swung themselves on large hooks gouged in the flesh, and burned widows on the funeral pyres of their husbands.

After learning the language, William enthusiastically began speaking to the Indian people about the Lord. But India was a spiritually dark and hard place. Seven years passed before the first convert! Slowly thereafter, the church began to grow.

In spite of huge personal sorrows—Carey lost two wives and a son prematurely—Carey used his gifts as a linguist to participate in translating all or part of the Bible into thirty-four different languages. He was extremely devoted to helping the Indian people in all ways that would benefit them. Among his achievements were advancement in agriculture and horticulture, the opening of a printing press, the introduction of the first steam engine in India, and the start of paper manufacturing on a large scale.

Perhaps his most important achievement for Indian culture was to fight Suti—the practice of burning widows so that, according to their heathen beliefs, they could go on to the spirit world to assist their husbands. Carey fought the practice for thirty-five years and not long before his death was overjoyed when the British colonial government finally banned.

Although Carey accomplished much in his lifetime for the cause of Christ, his achievements often were not flashy or quick in coming. He actually considered himself a plodder—day in and day out; he faithfully took one step at a time. There is a lesson in that for those of us who want results now.

I have visited Calcutta and have been to the Carey church. Although the Indian people still struggle with pagan religions, the light of the Lord Jesus shines in this vast land. It was Carey's convincing plea to preach the Gospel that every generation needs to seize in order to advance the Name of Jesus Christ.

Carey never returned to England. For more than forty years, he gave himself to the Indian people and his adopted country. He was a humble man. Just before his death in 1834, William told a friend, "You have been saying much about Dr. Carey and his work. After I am gone, please speak not of Dr. Carey, but rather of my wonderful Savior."[19]

DAVID LIVINGSTONE

Over the years, through my work with Samaritan's Purse, I have crisscrossed Africa in commercial and missionary aircraft. As you look down on that vast land of jungle, savanna, desert, and mountains, you cannot help but wonder, how did Livingstone cross this on foot? Without modern navigation tools and motorized transportation, just how did he do it?

Certainly one of the great representatives of Jesus Christ of all time was the missionary doctor and explorer David Livingstone. Born in Scotland in 1813, David grew up in a godly family. As a youth, he worked twelve-hour days in a cotton mill, studying the Bible and other books as he sat at the spinning wheel. After receiving training as a medical doctor, he heard the great missionary Dr. Robert Moffat from Africa speak. During the message, the Holy Spirit ignited a flame of zeal for the unsaved in young David's heart when he heard Dr. Moffat say, "I have sometimes seen, in the morning sun, the smoke of a thousand villages, where no missionary has ever been."[20]

David Livingstone said: "I am willing to go anywhere provided it is forward."

This vision of a wild, largely unexplored continent filled with people who had never heard of the Lord Jesus motivated Livingstone the remainder of his life.

David sailed to Africa in 1841 and after arriving immediately boarded an ox wagon for a seven-hundred-mile trip to a mission station. He then traveled to a more remote village and settled among the Bakwena tribe—the "people of the crocodile." In six months, David had mastered the language well enough to converse and preach the Gospel, leading many to Christ.

Livingstone always had a hunger to bring the Gospel to remote places never before visited by any foreigner, much less a missionary. As he forced his way through jungles, plains, and deserts in his ox cart, crowds often swarmed near to seek healing from "the White Doctor."

Every day brought life-threatening danger. At a place called Mabotsa, he found the villagers terrified by a large population of lions. David concluded that if he could kill one lion, the others probably would leave the sheep and cattle of the village alone. Livingstone took his gun in hand, and with several villagers armed with spears, sought out a huge lion resting behind foliage. David fired with both barrels, but as he paused to reload, the wounded lion charged, grabbed Livingstone by the shoulder, and shook him like a rag doll, shredding his arm and crushing his bone. Several natives rushed toward the beast, which distracted the animal into dropping the missionary. Before anyone was killed the lion fell, but David's arm never fully healed, leaving him with restricted movement and pain the rest of his life.

While in Africa, David married the daughter of a missionary. They continued their evangelism efforts together, and even with family responsibilities, David did not stop seeking to bring the Good News of Christ to distant tribes. After the Livingstones had three children, the entire family sought to cross the Kalahari Desert—one of the most punishing landscapes on earth. In one desolate section they did not see any sign of life, and with their water supply gone, for four days they pushed ahead, the children crying out in thirst. With everyone desperately ill, Livingstone was forced to turn back. One of the children died because of this ordeal.

Because of such terrible risks, David decided to send his family back to England, knowing that it might be years before he saw them again.

His family safe, Livingstone began a series of explorations into other unknown parts of vast Africa. Repeatedly he ventured into the interior jungles where no white man had ever walked. On one extended journey, during which David battled swarms of mosquitoes, encountered beasts and angry savages, and fell sick to fever thirty-one times, he and his guides traveled for six months to complete a fifteen-hundred-mile journey to the opposite coast. Then, after a short stay, they turned around and went back!

Having traveled in the same region in a Land Rover, I find it nearly incomprehensible that Livingstone walked much of the same territory. This certainly was a man passionately committed to the spread of the Gospel. He once said, "Cannot the love of Christ carry the missionary where the slave trade carries the trader?"

More than any other factor, it was the evil of the African slave trade that broke David Livingstone's heart to the point that he was willing to die himself to see "captives set free."

After five years of exploration and spreading the Gospel, Livingstone finally sailed home to see his wife, Mary, and family. Taking just a few months of rest and recovery, David, Mary, and their youngest son returned to Africa. Mary's health never was strong enough for the harsh conditions, and after a brief illness she died and was buried in the African wilderness. Even in his grief, Livingstone never abandoned his vision to conquer Africa for the Name. After one more visit to England to see his children and rally support against the slave trade, he returned to Africa—where at Zanzibar he visited a slave market. There he saw three hundred Africans penned up waiting for sale, with three hundred more arriving in town.

Once again, he marched into the interior. Livingstone saw the slave trade as one of the evils of his day. On one occasion, he encountered a long line of adults and children chained together, the armed slave drivers herding them like animals to the slave market. When the traders saw Livingstone, knowing of his fierce opposition to their business, they ran into the jungle. This brave missionary then had the joy of cutting the chains from eighty-four slaves and setting them free. Later he would share the Gospel with many of them and see them receive the ultimate freedom from their spiritual slavery to sin.

On Livingstone's fifty-ninth birthday he wrote in his journal, "My Jesus, my King, my All; I again dedicate my whole self to Thee." Less than two months later David became very ill. In a tiny village, deep in the continent he loved so much, Livingstone fell to his knees to pray, as was always his practice. That is how his African friends found him on May 4, 1873—still on his knees. He had gone to be with the Lord as he poured out his love for Africa with his final breath.

The Africans embalmed his body for its long journey back to England. No doubt aware of Livingstone's wishes, though, they removed his heart and buried it in African soil. Nearly a year later his remains were laid to rest with great honor at Westminster Abbey in London, the burial site of kings, queens, and heroes of Britain.

Although Livingstone the explorer never did find the source of the Nile, as he had hoped, during his estimated twenty-nine thousand miles of trekking throughout Africa, he discovered Victoria Falls in the four important lakes, and a number of rivers. His reports added about one million square miles of territory to the known world.

Livingstone's greatest legacy, though, is as one who advanced the Name of Jesus Christ, as no one else had, to a continent desperately in need of the Gospel's light. Livingstone once said, "I am a missionary heart and soul. God had an only Son and He was a Missionary. I am a poor imitation, but in this service I hope to live, and in it I wish to die."[21]

ELEANOR SOLTAU

Most people have heard of William Carey and David Livingstone, but a great woman of the faith, Eleanor Soltau, labored faithfully more recently with a nearly forgotten people in relative anonymity.

I am proud to say that Eleanor was a close friend of mine. I am sure that many of her prayers were a factor in turning my heart back to Christ when I was living in rebellion thirty years ago.

Eleanor was the daughter of missionary parents in what is now North Korea. She and my mother met when they were both students at the same school for children of missionaries in Korea.

Both girls attended Wheaton College in Illinois. After graduating, Eleanor went on to medical school. At some point, she became convinced that the Lord was calling her to become a missionary to the Bedouin tribespeople of the Middle East—not the most exciting place to go as a woman. Eleanor was obedient and with great enthusiasm went to Jordan in the mid-1950s to practice medicine.

In the 1960s she was asked to pioneer development of a new hospital in Jordan's northern desert at a desolate place called Al Mafraq, a village made of mud-brick buildings.

Once Eleanor settled in Jordan, she left behind her attachments to other lands and cultures. She fully identified with her new people by learning their language and immersing herself in their culture and customs.

That is how she served and gave herself to the advance of the greatest message of all time for nearly forty years.

As Eleanor approached retirement, she never considered leaving and going anywhere else. Her life had been expended for these people. Why leave now? Jordan was home.

Although in her seventies, Eleanor had too much energy left not to continue serving people. Therefore, she abandoned the idea of retirement and moved to southern Jordan where she started a new hospital!

A short time later, the Lord took Eleanor home to be with Him.

Eleanor's death created news in the Middle East. Ministers of the Jordan government, church leaders from throughout the country, members of the royal family, and hundreds of the common people to whom Eleanor had given her life attended her funeral. This honor was bestowed on a Christian woman in a heavily Muslim country, a lady who decades earlier had left all behind in order to advance the cause of Christ.

* * *

These saints gave their best to respond to the call, "Go therefore and make disciples." Yet more people are alive today than ever before, and they need to accept the saving knowledge of the Lord Jesus Christ.

10

INVESTING

"To win the cup, you have to become one with the sea."

I was incredibly intrigued by this statement and the man who said it.

Recently, I was invited to speak at a meeting of philanthropists gathered at an exclusive club in Palm Beach, Florida. A number of well-known individuals were seated at my table including a gentleman, a sailor, who had captained the boat that once won the most prestigious sailing competition in the world—the America's Cup. His name is Bill Koch.

In the early 1990s, sailors from the United States were eager to retain the America's Cup at the races to be held in 1992. Although active as a sailor for some years, Mr. Koch had not competed at this level before. I asked him a question that revealed some stunning insights into the cost of doing anything well: "How do you prepare to win the America's Cup?"

"Our boat was in the water and we practiced sailing for eighteen months, ten to twelve hours a day, seven days a week," Mr. Koch answered. "During the entire practice period only on Christmas day did the boat not sail. The daily routine did not vary. Everyone rose at 6 A.M. for two hours of exercise, preparation, and breakfast. This was followed by an hour of planning for the day's practice. At about 9 A.M., the boat set sail and stayed in the water on the practice course for ten hours, returning to dock at 7 P.M. Boat cleanup took one hour. Dinner was at 9 P.M. By 10 P.M., an exhausted crew turned in for the night. The next day the routine started all over again. Because of the rotation of backup crew members, about every ten days each crew member had one day off."

During my conversation with Mr. Koch, he told about the triumph of his team in winning the 1992 America's Cup.

Even with this level of preparation, his boat was considered a 100 to 1 long shot. Mr. Koch had no skill and his crew included several who had no sailing experience. However, he did have success in the business arena using what he called the "T3" approach, which stood for *teamwork*, *technology*, and *talent*. Bill Koch once wrote that the "glue that holds a team together is a clear focus."[1]

One reason Mr. Koch and his crew practiced so long on the actual racecourse was to understand the peculiar wind patterns in the area. "The winds have to work for you," he said, "but you have to know them to take advantage."

Then Mr. Koch said something I will never forget: "To win the cup, you have to become one with the sea."[2]

As I reflected on the incredible amount of commitment, training, and teamwork that he and his crew had exhibited to win a great prize, I was reminded of the Apostle Paul, who said, "I press on, that I may lay hold of that for which Christ Jesus has also laid hold of me . . . I do not count myself to have apprehended; but one thing I do, forgetting those things which are behind and reaching forward to those things which are ahead, I press toward the goal for the prize of the upward call of God in Christ Jesus."[3]

It takes more than boldness, bravery, and blood to make the Name of Jesus known throughout the earth. We must be willing to invest our most valuable resources and expend consistent, intense effort to advance His Name to the ends of the earth.

THE MASTER INVESTOR

Have you ever considered the number of people who have lived in the past twenty-plus centuries? Theoretically, how many actually stand between you and Jesus Christ?

Would you answer millions—maybe billions?

I admit this is something of a trick question. My answer is: About forty people separate you from Jesus! Here is my logic:

About two thousand years have passed since Christ came to redeem this earth back to His Father. If the average life expectancy of an individual over those centuries is fifty years, that means just forty people separate us from the time of Christ.

We know that most people—by a huge margin—come to Christ through the witness of another person. It often is a parent, close friend, work associate—or even a speaker or evangelist—who presents the Gospel.

This means that if the records existed on earth, you and I could come up with a list of about forty people who would be our ancestors, tracing back to the time of Jesus Christ and His apostles. This is why every believer must take seriously the responsibility Jesus gave His followers:

> And Jesus came and spoke to them, saying, "All authority has been given to Me in heaven and on earth. Go therefore and make disciples of all the nations, baptizing them in the name of the Father and of the Son and of the Holy Spirit, teaching them to observe all things that I have commanded you; and lo, I am with you always, even to the end of the age." Amen.[4]

"Go" really means, "Go invest yourself in others, who in turn will do the same." This model was put in place by Jesus—the Master—investing Himself in others.

At the beginning of His ministry, Jesus selected twelve men to train for His team. These recruits were not extraordinary; most of them were average men, but these fellows knew how to work. The Lord knew that anyone working for Him would have to be willing to work overtime. That has not changed!

The early followers of Jesus were more than just the Twelve. There were many disciples (followers of Jesus Christ) then, just as there are today. Those who followed Jesus included professional people like Dr. Luke, a physician; Matthew, a tax collector; even Nicodemus, a Pharisee who was one of the chief religious leaders in Jerusalem. Some of these disciples were open and public; others were discreet.

Jesus' strategy was to take adequate time—three years—to train His disciples by example. He instructed them through His preaching and teaching, and engaged them in one-on-one personal encounters in which He confronted, encouraged, and comforted. When Jesus determined His disciples were ready, He tested them by sending them out two-by-two on field trips so they could learn how to minister on their own. The Twelve did not travel together, but paired off and went in different directions.

In the process, the disciples had successes, but they also experienced failures. This was all part of the learning process, and they knew that when they got into trouble they could turn to Christ, just as we can today.

When Jesus' earthly mission was nearly completed, His disciples were ready to continue His ministry. Well, "ready" is a stretch. After their embarrassing inability to stay awake while Jesus prayed with agony in the Garden of Gethsemane, they deserted Jesus en masse when He was arrested. Jesus did not give up on them, though. He reappeared after His resurrection and showed great faith in His men by entrusting to them the Great Commission. He did warn them that they lacked just one thing: the presence and power of the Holy Spirit. This they received at Pentecost, which was like a great commissioning service for what would become the mightiest army ever seen in the history of mankind—the church.

Then these chosen and anointed men trained by Jesus carried the hope of the Cross, the message of salvation, and the power of the

Resurrection to the ends of the known earth, all in His mighty Name. This was possible because the disciples had become one with Christ.

Just think of the people—parents, friends, pastors, relatives, teachers—who have invested themselves in us.

Growing up, I remember how my mother would not let us kids go outside to play on Sunday afternoon until we could recite a Scripture verse from memory. As a father, I did similar things with my own children.

My parents have been an example to me all of my life. I watched my father, for instance, and saw no inconsistencies between his private and public life. That made an impact on me. When the great western actor, John Wayne, passed away, one of his sons was quoted as saying, "The John Wayne that the world saw on the silver screen was the same John Wayne we saw at home." That is true of my father. The Billy Graham that the world has seen in public is the same Billy Graham that I saw at home.

When I was a boy, John Rickman, a man who helped around our home, invested in my life by teaching me how to fish and hunt. How would I have known how to do this if someone had not shown me? The same applies in our spiritual life. We need to learn from those who have gone before us. One generation needs to teach the next generation.

When I was a teenager, a man by the name of Henry Holley, a retired Marine Master Sergeant, came to help my father organize evangelistic crusades. He spent hours investing in me and teaching me how to memorize Scripture. I was not a great student for Henry, but it is something that has stayed with me through the years. Naturally, my parents and family made a major investment in me, but there is a long list of individuals who have also invested in my life at different stages: my boyhood pastor, Dr. Calvin Thielman; when I was a teenager it was David Lee Hill; Dr. Roy Gustafson; and in my early ministry it was people like Dr. Bob Pierce, Dr. Robert Thompson, and Rev. Guy Davidson. When I began preaching, Dr. John Wesley White was a great help and encouragement to me. All of these great men shared their time with me, showed interest in me, and motivated me to do the same—invest in others.

We see that Jesus' followers had learned the "invest-in-people" lesson well.

This principle works in every generation. The Apostle Paul, for example, was always training people. He would arrive in a new city, share the Gospel and gather converts, establish a church, and train leaders. Then he would move on and repeat the process at a new place. However, he kept in touch with the churches through letters and return visits. The prayer, nurturing, and training never stopped.

The principle of investing in people applies in every area of life including the workplace. At Samaritan's Purse we train people not only to do their jobs but to do other tasks as well. It is an investment that costs us time and money, but the rewards are worth it because people have been trained and cross-trained, and we know that at all times people are prepared to get the job done.

When I first became involved in the ministry of Samaritan's Purse, there were just two employees—a secretary and me. The two of us worked together to do what needed to be done. In order to grow, though, we eventually had to bring in others and train them. Today, the ministry has expanded to more than 350 people at our international office alone.

My mother and father felt so strongly about investing in people that they built a training center in North Carolina called the Billy Graham Training Center at the Cove, a ministry of the Billy Graham Evangelistic Association. My mother was really the first to have this vision. After years of waiting and laying the idea before the Lord in prayer, the Cove opened in 1988 with the goal of training men and women in the Scripture and the techniques of evangelism. About forty seminars are offered there each year to train evangelists, pastors, and laypeople to be soul winners in their homes, churches, and businesses so that the Gospel will be passed on to others. The Cove also serves as the home for all the training ministries of the Billy Graham Evangelistic Association worldwide.

Making the Name of Jesus Christ known requires investment and training and the investment of our lives in His service.

WHAT WILL #41 DO?

If just 40 people separate us from Jesus Christ, that makes us number 41. Will we carry our responsibilities and make our mark in this rich heritage of faith?

I thank God for the thousands who sacrificed—at times their very blood—to make sure as many as possible could know the Lord Jesus. I am concerned that the fervor for evangelism is cooling in many hearts. If the Great Commission is to be carried out and the Name of the Lord Jesus Christ shared with every nation, our generation, too, must find its way to the dark corners of the world that still exist.

Not long ago I was reading the account of King Solomon when work was completed on the temple in Jerusalem. Solomon told the story of how his father, David, had really wanted to build the temple: "It was in the heart of my father David to build a temple for the name of the LORD God of Israel."[5] But Solomon points out that God did not want David to build the temple—that task would be Solomon's. I find it interesting that Solomon tells us that even though God did not allow David to accomplish this important task, He did commend David for having the desire to do a great work for the Lord. God told David, "You did well in that it was in your heart."[6]

Are the unsaved of the world on your heart?

God is very interested in our hearts' motives. It is in the heart where compassion for the lost and hurting grows. As David found out, not everyone is given the opportunity to do some great, specific task for His Kingdom. However, God wants us to have the vision for such great advances in our hearts. If we are to wear proudly the number "41," commitment is critical.

I admire the desires of my mother's heart as a young woman. Growing up, she had longed to give her life as a single, lifelong missionary to the people of Tibet. After high school in North Korea at a missionary school, she went to Wheaton College in Illinois to prepare.

Then my father came along and . . . well, she never got there. She determined that she needed to set aside her desire to go to Tibet as a missionary and instead become a helpmate to my father—but she still had the vision for Tibet "in her heart." I know that pleased God. Then, as a behind-the-scenes support for my father and his ministry, she did participate in sending the Gospel to the ends of the earth—probably even into the "closed-to-the-Gospel" country of Tibet.

A vision for bringing the Gospel to the unreached areas of the world was in the hearts of what is now called the "World War II generation." When our soldiers, sailors, marines, and airmen returned from duty posts all over the world, they brought with them a new understanding of the spiritual needs in foreign lands. As they shared their stories, a new generation was inspired to go as missionaries, and even many former servicemen and women went abroad to invest the rest of their lives to help accomplish the Great Commission.

Do we bear a similar passion in our generation?

Today, we have new tools to help spread the Name of the Lord Jesus Christ. Evidence of this became perhaps the most dramatic event in my father's international ministry. Using a crusade in San Juan, Puerto Rico, as a base, in March 1995 an outreach called Global Mission made use of satellite technology to beam the Gospel to nations that contained 70 percent of the world's population. Each day twenty-two hours of continuous transmission went out across twenty-nine time zones. Broadcasts were fed to three thousand venues in 185 countries and territories around the globe and interpreted into 117 languages ranging from A (Albanian) to Z (Zulu). In the receiving countries, the taped broadcasts were shown on jumbo screens at the appropriate time of day in large venues. People heard the Gospel in every conceivable setting—including refugees in a camp in Rwanda.

This satellite technology and other innovations like the Internet provide exciting opportunities. These methods need to be fully utilized to advance the Good News that Jesus died to redeem sinners. They do not replace the need for "foot soldiers" for the Gospel to set off on a missionary journey, like the Apostle Paul or David Livingstone. Millions of people still have never heard the Name of Jesus. The remote places of the earth will not be penetrated by the Gospel in any meaningful way by radio, TV, or e-mail alone. When the Lord Jesus said, "Go and make disciples of all nations," going is exactly what He meant.

In our day, we need an explosion of revived fervor for the advancement of the Gospel to every nation. I am thankful that something of this nature appears to be occurring among the "next generation," but we need passionate bearers of the Gospel from every age category. Although short-term mission trips and efforts are valuable, we need thousands willing to set off for foreign lands without concern about when—or if—they might return, as my grandfather did when he went to China in 1916.

Followers of the Lord Jesus need some of the radical zeal of the early Spanish explorer Hernán Cortés. Intent on conquering the Aztec Indians who ruled in what is now Mexico, in 1519 Cortés landed his fleet of eleven ships near present-day Veracruz. Some of his men showed something less than enthusiasm for a march inland, so Cortés set ten of his ships on fire. The message was clear: There is no turning back. "If necessary we will die here to accomplish our objectives. Retreat is not an option."[7]

When Christ gave the Great Commission, His faithful and loyal followers did "go" to all nations at that time. They did not look back in doubt of their mission. It is a good reminder to recall just how committed they were to the message they were sent to proclaim.

James, son of Zebedee, was killed with a sword under the rule of Herod Agrippa. He was the first of the Twelve to experience martyrdom.

John, son of Zebedee, was exiled by Rome to the Isle of Patmos, where he received the vision that became the book of the Revelation.

It is believed that Thomas took the Gospel east through what is known today as Iraq, Iran, Afghanistan, Pakistan, and then into India, and he was killed while engaged in missionary work in India.

Simon, tradition has it, was crucified in Egypt.

Mark was thought to have preached in Egypt and was burned to death there for his faith.

Simon (also known as Peter), after preaching the Gospel from Africa to Britain, is traditionally believed to have been crucified upside down because he did not feel worthy to die in the same manner as the Lord Jesus.

Bartholomew is believed to have preached in India. He was beaten, crucified, and beheaded in Armenia.

Andrew, Peter's brother, labored in the area north of the Black Sea in what is now Russia. Tradition says that he was crucified at Patrae, in Archaia.

Matthew ministered in Ethiopia and Egypt, where it is believed he was killed with a spear.

Philip preached in Asia Minor where he was reportedly stoned and crucified.[8]

Then the disciples gave their lives to spread the Gospel, and. by the time they died, the Name of the Lord Jesus Christ was known throughout the ancient world.

To win the world for Christ, we will have to invest everything—even our very lives. Are you willing? Will you seek to become one with our Lord?

Jesus said in Matthew, "From the days of John the Baptist until now, the kingdom of heaven has been forcefully advancing, and forceful men lay hold of it."[9] The force that He is speaking of is not a military force, not a force of coercion, but a very different kind of force: the force of unconditional love and sacrifice.

Think of the human emotion of love: the love a young man has for a young woman; the love a soldier has for a fellow comrade, to throw his body on top of another to save his friend's life. In Sarajevo, the capital of Bosnia during the civil war, there was a young man who crossed from the Muslim to the Serbian sector of the city to see the girl he loved. A sniper caught him and he died on a bridge. The girl came to his body, the sniper killed her, too, and his body lay clutched in her arms.

The Bible says, "Greater love has no one than this, that he lay down his life for his friends."[10] The force that is advancing the Name is love. Jesus said, "By this all men will know that you are my disciples, if you love one another."[11] The Gospel is advancing because of God's great love for you and me.

Think of the investment that God has made in you and me. We are His creation. That's a monumental investment. Tragically, this human family that we are part of was lost in sin and separated from His presence. God made another huge investment—to redeem us. He sent His only Son to pay the debt of sin for you and me. What a price—a debt that we can never repay. The greatest investment one can make is to become "one with Him," the One who possesses the greatest Name of all time.

11

FREEDOM FIGHTER

Jesus is the all-time "freedom fighter." Faith in Him and Him alone sets us free from the power of bondage and sin. If you want to be free, follow the Name. That was the challenge that He gave to all, even to this very day. On the Sabbath, in His hometown of Nazareth, Jesus stood in the synagogue and delivered the "declaration of independence" for all of mankind:

> And He was handed the book of the prophet Isaiah. And when He had opened the book, He found the place where it was written:
>
> "The Spirit of the LORD is upon Me,
> Because He has anointed Me
> To preach the gospel to the poor;
> He has sent Me to heal the brokenhearted,
> To proclaim liberty to the captives
> And recovery of sight to the blind,

> To set at liberty those who are oppressed;
> To proclaim the acceptable year of the LORD."

> Then He closed the book, and gave it back to the attendant and sat down. And the eyes of all who were in the synagogue were fixed on Him. And He began to say to them, "Today this Scripture is fulfilled in your hearing."[1]

With these stunning words, Jesus not only declared that He was the fulfillment of Isaiah's prophecy concerning a coming Savior, but also promised to free people from everything that oppresses and enslaves the human race.

Jesus said, "Most assuredly, I say to you, whoever commits sin is a slave of sin. And a slave does not abide in the house forever, but a son abides forever. Therefore if the Son makes you free, you shall be free indeed."[2]

The Name of Jesus brings freedom and hope.

Whatever struggles you may face—handicap, weakness, fear, tragedy, or sickness—Jesus came to declare the Good News of hope, liberty, and victory.

Two thousands years have passed since Jesus Christ set His foot on this planet to set captives free. The work of the Holy Spirit continues to this day, freeing men and women from sin's hold on them. Jesus is the Liberator and there is eternal freedom in His Name!

A FAMILY FINDS FREEDOM

I personally know many people who have experienced the freedom Christ gives.

Friends of mine, Sharon and Raul, met while attending the same high school. Abused as a child by an alcoholic father, Raul, a martial arts student, was filled with unresolved anger. Raul was a time bomb waiting to explode. One night when he saw Sharon at a party with another guy, his temper flared and he beat the young man severely. The authorities gave Raul a choice between a jail term or military service. A war zone seemed to appeal to his temper and since the Vietnam War was raging, Raul chose the military.

Sharon, the daughter of missionaries, fell in love with Raul while in high school and wrote to him faithfully while he served in Vietnam. Raul did not fill Sharon in on all the details he was facing in Vietnam under the great pressure of combat.

The stress of the war and the gruesomeness of his assignment pushed Raul over the edge. Unable to face even one more patrol or operation, Raul threatened his captain if ordered to go into the bush again. Raul was sent to a military hospital for emotional restoration and was there six months. He eventually received an honorable discharge from the military and married Sharon soon after.

Sharon was a follower of Christ, but Raul wanted nothing to do with "religion." Sharon was ready to give up on her husband and her dream of having a happy family and Christ-centered home. He was still boiling over with anger and, because of his experiences in the war, now had even fewer reservations to use violence.

He returned to his studies of martial arts with Jimmy H-Woo and later opened his own studio to teach self-defense to others. Raul began barhopping—looking for fights and often finding them. He also became abusive to Sharon. Without realizing it, Raul had become a slave to the sins of his father.

After four years of enduring Raul's destructive behavior, Sharon was ready to give up and leave him. The family now included two sons, and though Sharon still deeply loved Raul, she did not want her sons to suffer the same abuse Raul had received from his father.

On a Sunday afternoon, Sharon packed her belongings, planning to pick them up after the evening church service. Raul came home and saw the suitcases in the hallway. He realized Sharon's intentions and was enraged. Overwhelmed, Raul decided the only solution was to kill his wife.

Raul grabbed his rifle and loaded it. Marking time until Sharon returned, he roamed the house, punching holes in the walls, shattering the glass in pictures, and knocking over shelves.

Raul slammed the rifle butt into the TV, but instead of breaking the picture tube, he hit the power button. A preacher, Pastor Chuck Smith, was talking about Jesus and His redeeming love. This was the last thing Raul wanted to hear, so he stepped back and pointed the barrel, intending to blow the screen to pieces. But he just could not pull the trigger.

Raul felt Pastor Chuck was speaking directly to him. The Word of God is like a sword, and Raul felt the truth cutting through all the hardened layers covering his heart. Tears poured from his eyes. He put the rifle aside and knelt down before the television and prayed, "God, if You are real, and if You are a God who is able to save people, I want You to come into my life tonight." Immediately, peace settled in Raul's heart. When he stood to his feet, he knew a major change had taken place.

Raul unloaded the rifle and put it back in the closet. He figured Sharon was probably at church so he climbed into his car to make his way there. He rehearsed just what he would say to Sharon. As he arrived, the pastor was giving the altar call. Raul looked for Sharon but she had left the service early. As he stood listening to the pastor's urging, he walked to the altar and asked for prayer.

In the meantime, Sharon arrived home and found the house wrecked, confirming in her heart that it was time for her and the children to leave. She bolted the door until she could collect her thoughts, only to be interrupted by Raul's persistent knocking at the door.

"Sharon, open the door," Raul said in desperation.

With reluctance, Sharon cracked the door and asked, "What do you want?"

"I accepted Jesus Christ!" he said.

Not at all convinced, Sharon closed the door in his face. Living with an angry man, she had heard plenty of stories. Raul pleaded and finally convinced Sharon to open the door. She listened to him but remained skeptical. He managed to talk her into not leaving—at least not right away—and Sharon pondered his claim in her heart.

Days and weeks passed. Sharon saw changes in Raul but still wondered if he would turn back to his old ways.

Together they began attending a church, Calvary Chapel, and Sharon noticed that Raul showed an enormous hunger for the Bible. Sharon fully realized the depth of change in Raul when he started visiting their old high school to share the Gospel with the students. Just two months later, Raul stood on a bench at the school and explained how Jesus Christ had come to save the lost and offer freedom from anything that binds people in sin. Several hundred students responded to the Gospel and were saved! It was not long before Raul was visiting other high schools, proclaiming the same message and winning young people for the kingdom.

After many months of consistency, Sharon concluded that Raul was indeed a new man. She rejoiced that her prayers had been answered. The man she loved was forgiven of his sin through the power of the Lord Jesus Christ! Sharon, too, forgave Raul for all the pain he had caused her, and they began a new life together.

The Bible says: "Blessed are they whose transgressions are forgiven, whose sins are covered. Blessed is the man whose sin the Lord will never count against him."[3]

Raul started a Bible study at his martial arts studio. Years later he was ordained as a minister, and the Bible study grew into a large church. Sharon and Raul added a third son to their family, and today they continue to serve the Lord faithfully.

I have seen firsthand the power of God displayed in Raul's life and ministry. Many thousands have come to know Christ personally because of Raul's witness. He now pastors Calvary Chapel in Diamond Bar, a large church in southern California.

I asked his wife one day, "After Raul came to trust Jesus Christ as his personal Lord and Savior, how long did it really take you to fully comprehend that his life had changed?"

"A year," she answered. "During that first year I was afraid the old ugly head of violence, temper, and anger would come boiling out at any moment." She realized that his life indeed had changed and that he was not the same. He was a new man—a result of Christ's living in him.

When Jesus said he came to heal the brokenhearted, He was referring to people like Sharon, who had just about surrendered hope of ever experiencing a Christian marriage. Jesus was also thinking about others, like Raul, when He said that He would "proclaim liberty to the captives." Gone was Raul's enslavement to anger, alcohol, and violence. In its place was the freedom to live a life of peace that brings honor and glory to the Name of the One he faithfully serves.

A YOUNG MAN DISCOVERS HIS NAME

One of the plagues of our time is divorce. It has become so easy, so casual, so accepted, for a man and a woman to walk away from the vows they made before God, when they committed their lives to each other. All sorts of reasons are cited. In some cases, they are tragically justifiable, but many times the real reason for divorce is selfishness. Thinking chiefly of themselves, two people decide they are tired of the hard work that marriage requires, so they break up.

In the process, the children involved often suffer emotional wounds that, humanly speaking, are irreparable. Children of divorce sometimes go through the rest of their lives never sure whom they can trust, never knowing deep down that they are loved. They can become bound by fear and bitterness. Greg was a boy who came from such a background.

Greg had known four stepfathers by the time he was nine. On the exterior, his mother, with her stunning good looks, could pass for a movie star. However, on the inside she was empty. Her search for fulfillment led her from man to man, often in rapid succession, as she dragged Greg from house to house across America. She had little regard for the impact her lifestyle was having on him.

In an attempt to establish a permanent identity, he called himself by the last name of his fourth stepfather, who treated him kindly. Before long, his mother left this man and moved Greg on to another stepfather—only to leave that one also. After having his life repeatedly uprooted, and never really knowing the security of a stable family, Greg went into survival mode. He rebelled with determination against an adult world filled with deception and betrayal.

Greg descended into heavy drug use at a frightening pace. Like many in the counterculture of the '60s and '70s, Greg decided he would pursue truth and purpose through mind-altering drugs. First marijuana, then LSD, became his ticket out of the pain of his life, at least for as long as the highs lasted. The LSD especially ushered him into a realm filled with new "meaning."

About this time, Greg began to notice that some of the kids in his school were unashamed followers of the Name. In fact, some of them were students who had once, like him, used drugs. Now, they were handing him tracts and witnessing to him about Christ. Having been burned plenty of times before, though, Greg was not impressed.

He continued dabbling with LSD and one day took a particularly large dose. Rather than experiencing euphoria, Greg became keenly aware of the presence of evil. Feeling that he was losing control, and even his sanity, he stared into a mirror in an attempt to reconnect with reality. As he did, the image before him melted and he seemed to hear a hideous voice telling him, "You're gonna die!" In the days that followed, a shaken Greg tried to make sense of it all.

One day at school, Greg found himself standing on the fringe of a crowd listening to a former drug user talk about how the Lord Jesus Christ had changed his life, and how He could change theirs too. While Greg had no interest in becoming one of these "Jesus people"—as they were called in the early '70s in California—he did remember having prayed as a small boy asking for God's help. In spite of it, though, Greg continued living the same rebellious way. That day in school, however, Greg realized he could no longer play games with God. He either had to be for Him or against Him. He knew that by not standing for Jesus he actually was standing against Him.

Greg struggled inside. He wrestled with whether he could give up his lifestyle. In view of his family history, he also questioned whether he could trust anyone, let alone a God he could not see. Still, the message that God loved him so much that He gave His one and only Son for Greg rang in his heart. Greg bowed his head and invited Christ to be his Lord and Savior. The boy who had never really known an earthly father now had a heavenly Father. The young man who had never known for sure what name he should go by had now chosen to follow the Name above all names.

Greg became involved in a Bible study, and by the time he was nineteen, he was leading a Bible study of his own in the city of Riverside. That Bible study has grown into a church—one of the largest churches in America. Greg is on radio and television across the country and holds annual evangelistic crusades known as Harvest Crusades. I have known Greg for fifteen years and have seen God work in his life. He is a man who God is using in a unique way to touch the lives of thousands.

DELIVERED FROM EVIL

A different type of evil oppressed another young man.

Skip was in his mid teens when he and a friend began dabbling in psychic powers. While traveling with a high school tour group in Mexico, Skip and his friend separated themselves from the others and holed up in a hotel room in Mazatlan. From there, they hoped to contact the spirit world.

Skip's friend already had a reputation for reading people's fortunes with tarot cards. Now the two teenagers wanted the spirits to control them and send messages through "automatic writing."

After waiting in the hotel room for two nights, Skip was in a trance—asking the spirits to move his arm and write messages about what he believed were his past lives.

The damp night ocean air flowed in through the windows. The curtains flapped and an electric presence filled the air. Skip's arm started moving without his control. At first the pen scribbles were meaningless, but it wasn't long before words began to form: "You were in the Franco-Persian War where you were killed."

Convinced now that reincarnation must be true, Skip was exhilarated. If life consisted of just one existence after another, should he not experience each one and throw it away like a half-smoked cigarette? New thrills followed. Later, Skip, along with members of a rock band he played with, smoked huge amounts of Acapulco gold marijuana in a sealed-off practice room. One night Skip and a friend committed a crime and they were busted by the police for grand larceny, but Skip had no remorse; breaking the law exhilarated him.

By the time Skip was eighteen he was already burned out on life. He had tried everything, all the thrills of southern California, from drugs to surfing to rock and roll; he was bored and frustrated. The temporary thrills did not lead to happiness. The psychic experiments had only left him confused and empty.

One day Skip was alone watching TV, flipping through the channels, when a man addressing a large crowd in a packed stadium caught his attention. Skip was mesmerized as the speaker's blue eyes seemed to pierce his heart. For the first time, he heard the Gospel of Jesus Christ through the message given by my father, Billy Graham.

Skip sensed he was facing a choice that he wanted to avoid and started to turn off the TV, but something stopped him. He couldn't pull himself away as his heart pounded. Skip knew that if he were in the stadium he would be compelled to respond to the invitation. Instead, he was safe in the privacy of his home. No one was there to pressure him to make any decision . . . until the piercing eyes looked directly into the camera. "For those of you watching by television, wherever you are—in a bar, or a hotel room—you, too, can turn your life over to Jesus Christ."

Skip's stomach was in knots.

My father prayed, asking those who had responded to the invitation for God's forgiveness to repeat the prayer with him. Skip listened intently, but then quickly turned off the television and walked half-stunned to the bedroom. There, after mulling through the hallways of his past experiences and pondering the thought of a brand-new life, he fell to his knees and prayed. In a mere moment, what seemed like a million-pound weight lifted from his heart. Skip knew joy for the first time in his life.

As he grew in his new faith, he learned the biblical term for what had happened to him—he had been "born again." He understood that his soul had been washed and made new.

As Paul the Apostle was relating his conversion experience to King Agrippa, he said that Jesus sent him to the Gentiles to turn them from darkness to light, from the power of Satan to God.[4] This describes what happened to Skip. There is no life so dark that the light of Jesus cannot shine in, cleanse, and make all things new. The demonic spirits that once moved Skip's arm in the Mazatlan hotel room could only offer him a message of death. The One who bears the Name of Jesus Christ offers life and liberty from the oppression of evil.

Several years passed, and Skip felt led by God to enter a church-planting ministry. In time, he married and moved to New Mexico to start a church. After early challenges and discouragement, God's blessings poured out on Skip's congregation. Today, Calvary Chapel of Albuquerque is the largest church in New Mexico, and one of the larger churches in the United States.

Raul Ries, Greg Laurie, and Skip Heitzig, through preaching the Gospel, impact people far beyond the four walls of their churches. Many throughout the evangelical world seek their advice and counsel. They are helping many people find freedom in the Name.

12

SERVING

After several years of watching how Jesus operated, His disciples still did not get the picture. Walking toward Jerusalem one day, not long before the events that ended Jesus' earthly life, James and John asked for a little perk for their service: "They said to Him, 'Grant us that we may sit, one on Your right hand and the other on Your left, in Your glory.'"[1]

Jesus had to set them straight: To follow Him did not guarantee prominence or an easy life. What Jesus told James and John probably shocked them: "Whoever desires to become great among you shall be your servant. And whoever of you desires to be first shall be slave of all. For even the Son of Man did not come to be served, but to serve, and to give His life a ransom for many."[2]

The message that Jesus proclaims continues to advance through the footsteps of His servants. When Jesus walked this earth, He cared about individual people and served them. As His representatives now, Jesus asks us to love others in the same way. He lived an example that we should follow. Two thousand years have passed, but God's instructions to those who follow Him have not changed.

Jesus exemplified the true meaning of serving others—even in caring for His mother. As Jesus was dying for the sins of mankind, His Father in heaven had to turn His back on His Son who bore the sins of the world. Amid the pain, agony, and shame while hanging on the cross, Jesus took time to remember His mother. He looked down at her and spoke to the disciple whom He loved, standing next to her, asking John to take care of her. John took Mary into his home and cared for her from that time on.[3]

Jesus cared for the "forgotten." He healed a crippled man who had been an invalid for thirty-eight years lying by the pool at the Sheep Gate in Jerusalem.[4] There was a woman who had suffered for twelve years who touched the hem of Jesus' cloak and was healed.[5] Jesus, the King of kings, in the midst of accomplishing the most important mission in history, noticed these forgotten ones and stopped to heal them.

Jesus cared for "the enemy." In the city of Capernaum, an officer of the powerful Roman military sought a favor. This centurion recognized the greater power that Jesus possessed. The centurion displayed such faith that Jesus commended him and responded to the man's plea to heal his servant.[6] Jesus cared for all those in need regardless of their status or circumstances.

Jesus cared for the despised. Probably the most despised person of Jesus' day was the tax collector; yet Jesus chose one of them, Matthew, to be a disciple. While visiting Jericho, Jesus was also a houseguest of Zacchaeus, another tax collector.

Jesus cared about children. In New Testament days, children were considered a blessing. He often used them to illustrate His teaching. One day, parents were bringing their children to Him for a touch and a prayer, but the disciples tried to shoo them away. Jesus stopped the disciples and said, "Let the little children come to Me, and do not forbid them; for of such is the kingdom of heaven."[7]

Jesus cared for the hungry. He once fed five thousand men plus women and children.[8] On another occasion, He fed four thousand.[9]

Jesus cared for the rich and the well-to-do. Jesus reached out to the lowly, but at the same time walked into the highest levels of society. He did not condemn the wealthy. When the rich young ruler came to Jesus and asked how he might find eternal life, Jesus listened patiently and "loved him." The man's status and wealth did not stir up prejudice in Jesus. He was attentive. The problem was not the young man's wealth, but his *love* and attachment to his wealth. Whatever comes between us and our relationship with Christ is sin. This young man loved his money more than his own soul.[10]

The Bible says, "For what will it profit a man if he gains the whole world, and loses his own soul?"[11] This young man had it all except for one thing: faith. He did not trust Jesus Christ as his Savior and was not willing to exchange his earthly wealth for treasures in heaven.

Jesus cared about single mothers. One day Jesus was so moved with compassion by a widow's plight that He performed a miracle for her. This woman's only son had died and the funeral procession was headed to the cemetery.

> When the Lord saw her, He had compassion on her and said to her, "Do not weep." Then He came and touched the open coffin, and those who carried him stood still. And He said, "Young man, I say to you, arise." So he who was dead sat up and began to speak. And He presented him to his mother.[12]

Jesus cared for annoying people. Some people just grate on your nerves—you want to run and hide when they call or pull you aside at the mall. The truth is that everyone at times can annoy somebody.

Jesus met His share of annoying people, but He loved and served them. One woman who was following Him and yelling to get His attention caused such a scene that the disciples asked Jesus if they could "send her away." Since the woman was a Caananite and not a Jew, Jesus told her that His mission was to the "lost sheep of Israel." But the woman would not take no for an answer. She was persistent. She believed in Him, and Jesus saw her faith. He granted her desire and healed her daughter. Jesus marveled at her faith.[13] The Lord Jesus said, "Come to Me, all you who labor and are heavy laden and I will give you rest."[14] This is exactly what He did even for a Canaanite.

Jesus cared for the demon-possessed. Demon possession is just as real as cancer. Demons disturb men physically, mentally, and spiritually. They can destroy souls and be the eternal doom of men. The Scripture tells us of an encounter that Jesus had with one such person. Talk about a guy who had problems—this man was possessed by demons and ran naked, and was often be chained up in a graveyard because he was so uncontrollable. His strength was such that he would break free and run about, screaming night and day. Jesus did not keep His distance and pass by. Jesus had compassion on him and cast out a multitude of demons. The man came to his senses, put his clothes on, and wanted to follow Jesus. But on this occasion, Jesus told him to return to his home and be a witness and testimony in his own town.[15]

Jesus cared for the condemned and guilty. Jesus was always reaching out to those around Him, even in death. He was crucified between two common criminals accused of stealing and condemned to death. They were guilty. One of them spoke to Jesus from the cross, believed, and asked Jesus to remember him when He came into His kingdom. Jesus recognized his faith and said, "Assuredly, I say to you, today you will be with Me in Paradise."[16]

Jesus had compassion for sinners and helped them unconditionally. No matter how disgusting, disenfranchised, or diseased they were, Jesus was willing to serve them right where they were—in the midst of great need—when they had no one else to whom they could turn. He is still reaching out to this very day.

REPRESENTING THE NAME

Through the work of Samaritan's Purse, I have encountered a steady stream of people who bring honor to the Name of the Lord by the way they represent Jesus in caring for people. I have had the privilege of meeting some of today's great men and women who serve others in His Name.

JOHN PHAM, VIETNAM

The Vietnamese call them *bui doi*—"the dust of life"—children of the streets, unwanted and unloved. As many as one hundred thousand children roam the jammed streets of Vietnamese cities with no one to care for them and no place to call home. Robbed of their childhood, this next generation falls victim to hunger, disease, abuse, and exploitation.

John Pham, a Vietnamese refugee who immigrated to Canada shortly after the Indo-China War thirty years ago, has reached out to the *bui doi* in the name of Jesus Christ. God led John back to Vietnam as a missionary to his own people. While John provides for the physical needs of the street children, with the help of Samaritan's Purse he shares with them the Good News of Jesus Christ.

One of the "least of these," Chung, was only eight years old when his father died and his mother deserted the family. Chung's teenage brother found work at a blacksmith's shop—melting down metal scraps left from the war—to support his younger brother and sister. Within a year, Chung's brother was killed when a grenade in the scrap metal exploded. Chung took his brother's place at the shop, toiling fifteen hours a day, until the work came to an end. He was unable to feed himself and his sister, so Chung came to Hanoi to work on the streets as a shoeshine boy.

Fortunately, Chung met John, who was able to rescue the boy from the horrors of street life and provide him with food, shelter, and medical care. Chung still shines shoes and sends money back home to his sister, but now he has good meals, a safe place to sleep, and lots of love from those who follow in the footsteps of Jesus.

TIA ANA, EL SALVADOR

Tia Ana is from the capital city of El Salvador, the only country in the world named for the Savior. As a young girl, she was abused by close family members and ran away from home at the age of seven. Once on the streets, she had to fight to survive. Her life continued to take turns for the worse as she engaged in illicit behavior, including prostitution.

Due to physical abuse, she was unable to have a child of her own. As the years passed and took their toll on her, she became desperate and cried out to God, asking Him if He were real, to save her from the life she was living. He did, and Tia Ana turned her life over to the Lord and began serving Him.

She so desperately wanted to have a child, but because of her past sin she knew she would never hold her very own child in her arms. Again, she sought the Lord and laid her burden before Him. "Lord," she said, "if You will just give me a child, I will raise that child to also serve You faithfully." Through the support and encouragement of her church, she began to minister to the people on the streets, in particular the children of prostitutes. In the process, the Lord did bring into her life a little orphan girl, and Ana began raising the child as her very own.

As time passed, Ana realized that there were so many children without parents. She noticed that the daycare centers downtown were closing, especially those that cared for the children of prostitutes, leaving these children to fend for themselves. Ana opened the doors of her home to feed and love these children.

Ana now runs a daycare center that ministers to approximately seventy-five children.

I met Ana while holding a crusade in San Salvador. Through our children's ministry, Operation Christmas Child, we were able to distribute gifts to each child in her home. Ana told me, "I try to give them the most important value of life: To have faith in the Name that is above all names—the Son of the Living God."

ELMER KILBOURNE AND EZRA SARGUNAM, INDIA

Next to China, India is the most populated nation on this planet, home to a billion people. Yet in a country with more than nine hundred million Hindus and Muslims, fewer than 1 percent are Christians. How does the church evangelize such multitudes?

Dr. Elmer Kilbourne served as a missionary leader in Korea for four decades and retired in 1985. He shared with me his burden to see India evangelized. "Franklin," he said, "I don't want to retire in

Florida to play shuffleboard. I would like my last years to count for something while I still have my health. Let's help the Evangelical Church of India build one thousand churches."

"Build one thousand churches in India?" I said. "You must be nuts!"

"Not just one thousand churches," Elmer replied. "I also want to help them build four seminaries and twenty-five Bible schools—one in each state. If we are going to build one thousand churches, we've got to train pastors to preach in them. What do you think?"

I just stared at him. I could not help but admire Elmer's faith and determination. I knew that such a monumental task could not be accomplished in our own strength—God would have to do a miracle. "Let's go," I said, "and watch God work."

I met with Dr. Ezra Sargunam, leader of the Evangelical Church of India (ECI). He, too, shared a powerful vision for reaching his nation for Christ. When I heard what he had to say, I knew that Elmer's dream was possible with God's help.

In the years since, the ECI—with the support of a small consortium of businesses, mission groups, and concerned individuals—has seen God do a miracle. A team from Samaritan's Purse participated in "Festival One Thousand" as the ECI celebrated the completion of the one-thousandth church. The highlight of the festival was the mass baptism of 2,231 new converts to the Christian faith—the largest group ever baptized in India during the twentieth century. These new Christians came from all over India, and it took twenty pastors a good part of the day to baptize them all.

Despite this wonderful victory for God's Kingdom, India remains in great spiritual darkness. On the same day that these new believers were baptized, millions of Hindus rushed to immerse themselves in the Ganges River, believing that the water would wash away their sins. It is sad to think of people believing that one of the world's most heavily polluted rivers could somehow wash away their guilt and penalty of sin. As the old hymn says: "What can wash away my sins? Nothing but the blood of Jesus."

The ECI has a plan to challenge every local church to plant a sister church in the next few years. The goal is to plant another one thousand churches by the year 2010. With Elmer's enthusiasm, Ezra's vision, and God's blessing, I consider this a "done deal"!

All of these faithful servants and millions like them across the globe, through simple obedience, set the needs of others above their own. In doing so, they join the ranks of those who have served and cared for others in the Name.

13

REACHING THE STRANGER

"For the LORD your God is God of gods and Lord of lords, the great God, mighty and awesome, who shows no partiality . . . He administers justice for the fatherless and the widow, and loves the stranger, giving him food and clothing. Therefore love the stranger."[1]

In our ministries at Samaritan's Purse and the Billy Graham Evangelistic Association, I am humbled every day by the generosity of thousands of self-sacrificing individuals who make our relief and evangelism work possible throughout the world. But even I was surprised by the spirit of generosity of God's people through our children's project known as Operation Christmas Child.

It was August 1993, at the height of the war in Bosnia, when I received a call from a man in England. He said that he was taking gift-filled shoeboxes to children in Bosnia that Christmas. There were literally hundreds of thousands of refugees scattered throughout the Balkans. Cities had been destroyed, homes burned, and families had experienced "ethnic cleansing." It was a mess! The man from England asked if we could help. I assured him that we would.

That summer we were extremely busy. To be honest, it wasn't long before I forgot my promise. September and October passed. It was mid-November when another call came from England. The man asked how many shoeboxes we had collected. He was preparing to go to Bosnia the next month. *Shoeboxes?* I thought. Then it dawned on me, the promise I had made had been forgotten. Not wanting to disappoint him, I told him we would get back in touch in a few days. He was satisfied that we were on top of it, but when I hung up, I was in a panic. I tried to figure out how we might collect thousands of boxes in just a few short weeks.

I called a pastor who serves on my board of directors, Dr. Ross Rhoads, and presented my dilemma to him. "Ross," I asked, "would you be willing to present this project to your church and ask if they would fill some shoeboxes with toys for children in Bosnia?" He agreed.

To my surprise, a couple of weeks later he called and reported that the church had collected nearly eleven thousand boxes. "What should I do with them all?" Ross asked. I was stunned. These boxes had been collected by strangers—to give to strangers—halfway around the world.

We went to Bosnia to help distribute the shoeboxes and saw the incredible impact these gifts had on the children—to us, strangers—who had only known war, bloodshed, and destruction. For the first time in their young lives, they had a moment of joy and a glimpse of hope.

Now the challenge: How do we take this idea of giving gifts to total strangers—children—and make this an evangelistic project to where we communicate the Gospel to every child? The next year the project more than doubled. We went back to Bosnia, this time with teams of Christian laypeople—many of them strangers to me. They had heard about the project and wanted to be part of it. They were willing to risk their lives in this war zone. Our team took every opportunity to tell the children about God's love, His Son, Jesus Christ. We went to schools, refugee camps, and hospitals. Families were overwhelmed and grateful for what had been done for their children. In the midst of their darkest hour, it gave them a moment of reprieve from insurmountable suffering.

What makes this project unique is that families—strangers to these children—fill these boxes. I do not know the theology of praying for a box of toys, but we ask people as they pack the boxes to pray that God will guide and direct their gift into the hands of the right child so that it will not only provide joy but also be a witness for the true Christmas Child.

In 2001, more than five million shoebox gifts were collected. Can you fathom having millions of people praying for millions of children to come to know Christ? We know that God will hear the prayers of the righteous who pray for the salvation of children. Our God is a giving God.

We also ask those packing the boxes that they put their picture in the box and perhaps even a letter to encourage the child overseas to write back. Our hope is that through the years, we will be able to build bridges of friendship between children around the world and families from the giving countries.

A few years ago, I was speaking at Calvary Chapel in Albuquerque, New Mexico. It was a special Sunday in December dedicated to Operation Christmas Child. Each year, this church collects in excess of fifteen thousand boxes. A woman brought a shoebox that she had carefully packed. With tears in her eyes, she told how in the early 1990s she was in a refugee camp in Bosnia and a "stranger" gave her one of our shoeboxes. For the first time in her life, that young girl experienced a little joy and hope that there was someone who loved her. She is now a young woman attending the University of New Mexico and has come to know Jesus Christ as her personal Lord and Savior. When I hear a story like this, my heart leaps within, and I cannot help but say, "Thank You, Father!" Does prayer work? You bet it does!

My good friend from Beirut, Sami Dagher, who has helped us distribute shoeboxes throughout Lebanon, shared with me this story: A Muslim family in Beirut was searching for a copy of the Bible. They had seen another family with a copy of a children's Bible, and wanted one for their son. When Sami, along with our Operation Christmas Child team, did a distribution of shoeboxes in a Lebanese school, that little boy opened his shoebox and found a copy of the Bible in the Arabic language.

Can you imagine God directing a family to put a Bible in Arabic in their shoebox (not knowing where it was going), and out of five million boxes, theirs was packed, sent to a processing center, sealed and put onto a pallet, and then shipped in a container across the ocean, ending up in Beirut, Lebanon, of all places, and eventually in the hands of this little boy who wanted a Bible?

There is no way we can possibly manage to direct boxes to certain areas. In most cases, we normally ship boxes from the West Coast to Central and South America; boxes from the East Coast to Eastern Europe and Africa; and boxes from the Pacific Northwest to Asia. Somehow, through all of these processes, God has His plans.

There are dozens of stories like this. During the Kosovo war, tens of thousands of people were killed and hundreds of thousands were forced to flee into neighboring countries, in what the media called ethnic cleansing. It was reminiscent of the Holocaust in Nazi Germany.

As this drama was being played out, Samaritan's Purse responded by going into Albania. Within a few weeks, we were building a massive tent city for these refugees. During this process, we got to know many Kosovars personally. When the United States military intervened and the war came to an end, we went back with the returning refugees to their homes. For many there was not much left. Homes had been looted and burned, and farm animals were killed, but in this war-torn country we had an opportunity to show God's love.

That Christmas, I was in Kosovo distributing shoeboxes to schoolchildren. It was bitterly cold as we stood inside the unheated classroom. Here in Kosovo, as we always do at these distributions, we put a box into the hands of each child and asked that they hold them until everyone had received a gift. While the kids were holding their boxes with great anticipation, it gave me an opportunity to tell them where the gifts were from, why the gifts were sent, and share with them the Christmas story—about the greatest Giver of all, the Lord Jesus Christ. On the count of three, they were told they could open their boxes, and there was an outbreak of excitement filled with giggles, laughter, smiles, and joy. A girl pulled a doll from her box; a little boy found a truck in his; and I watched as one boy pulled out a deflated soccer ball—pump and all! We helped him pump it up and watched as he kicked that soccer ball all over the room. A million dollars would not have meant more to him than that gift.

In the midst of the thrill, I happened to notice another little boy open his box and quickly put the lid back on. He sat there with blue lips, shivering in the cold room. None of the children had warm clothing, certainly no hats or heavy coats. I went over thinking that he must have gotten a mismarked box; possibly for a girl; or perhaps there was little inside. I walked over to him and examined the box as the young boy's eyes followed my every move. As I lifted the lid, a T-shirt covered the rest of the contents, but it did not appear to have any toys, or anything else, that would excite a kid. But when I lifted the t-shirt, hidden underneath was a fleece-lined leather jacket. When I pulled it from the oversized shoebox and shook it out, the boy's eyes doubled in size. Quivering from the chills, he could hardly control his emotions. I unbuttoned the jacket and helped him put it on . . . it was a perfect fit. How did God know? These boxes had been packed by German Christians and sent from our office in Berlin. I believe that a family in Germany had been touched by God to put a leather jacket in that shoebox. Why? For a little boy in Kosovo—a direct result of the prayers of God's people.

Because of Operation Christmas Child and our evangelism, relief, and development work, since the war we have been able to help plant more than ten churches in Kosovo. The gifts, the love, and the relief work all come together to lift up the Name of Jesus Christ.

I mentioned earlier that we ask people to insert letters with return addresses, hoping that children will write back. Yet, there are children who do not have access to stamps; they are too poor and would not be able to send letters overseas, but on occasion it does happen. There are hundreds of stories about how God works through this project.

A few years ago, a family in Pennsylvania sent a shoebox in which their daughter, Lauren, included a letter. That box ended up in the Balkans in the country of Croatia. The little girl, Sanja, who received the box, wrote Lauren back six months later, and they became pen pals for four years. When the planes crashed into the World Trade Towers on 9/11, the news was instantly broadcast around the world.

Lauren's family received a phone call from Sanja's aunt (the only one who could speak English in the family). Lauren's father wrote to us:

> She [the aunt] expressed her concern for our family. I could hear the voices of the family in the background posing questions and comments in Croatian. I assured her that we were okay and asked her how they were doing. "We are fine," she said. "Everything is fine in Croatia; it is you and your family in America who we are worried about." Before we said good-bye, I told her that Lauren sent her love to Sanja, and that we pray for their family quite often. She thanked me and told me that they pray for us and now they would also be praying for all America. Why do we need to show others love? Jesus makes it very clear that the very love we give to others will someday be given back to us. Who could have ever thought that a poor and needy family from Croatia would one day be telephoning a family in the prosperous and peaceful United States offering words of concern, comfort, and prayer.

When I hear stories like this, there are no words to describe my amazement over the impact made on the lives of "strangers" by a simple shoebox and prayer. When prayers are lifted to God, in the Name of His Son, they are answered a hundredfold. That phone call to Lauren's family meant more to them than any other gift.

SMILES KNOW NO BORDERS

Operation Christmas Child makes a lot of people smile.

The grins begin when children go with their parents to the store to fill a shoebox with goodies for a child they will probably never meet. Then our volunteers at the collection/distribution centers break out in smiles when they see thousands of brightly wrapped boxes pouring in. Even our volunteers and staff in countries all over the world smile as they work with local church leaders to arrange the gift giveaways.

The most beautiful smiles are those that pop up on the faces of children in the remote areas around the globe when they hold their gifts. Many of them have never received a gift or even heard the Name of the One who gave Himself as the Greatest Gift.

We have enough stories to fill an entire book, but I want to give a few vignettes—glimpses into lives of those who have been touched and who have touched others through Operation Christmas Child in the Name of Jesus.

HONDURAS

A pastor writes:

> Membership in my church has tripled in the last three years simply because Operation Christmas Child has been a wonderful evangelism tool.

ASIA

Kazakhstan, a former Russian Republic, is now an independent country in Central Asia that borders Afghanistan.

One parent writes:

> My whole family and children love God. My oldest son is seven, and he can pray. When he heard about the gifts, he began to pray for running shoes. He had a strong faith. When we came to the church, he began to praise God because he was sure that he would get what he prayed for. When he opened the box, inside were running shoes. My son cried out aloud, "Thank You, Jesus!"

INDIA

A letter from a boy named Asim:

> I belong to the Muslim community. One day when I was playing with a Christian friend of mine, he told me that the gifts sent by American children were coming . . . I received my box and opened

> it to find toys, candy, a ball, and other American stuff. I felt very happy. I am grateful to the American children and Samaritan's Purse for the gift, as well as the opportunity to experience the real gift, Jesus Christ, in my life. I am now attending the church regularly and learning more about Jesus.

Another child writes:

> I was born and raised in a Hindu family. One of my friends who happens to be a Christian took me to the place where boxes were distributed to the poor. After this, I felt Jesus' love and I started attending the Sunday school. Today, after accepting Jesus, I am happy and I thank you and the American children for the valuable gift that you sent to me.

ARMENIA

One of our field staff reports:

> During our distribution in the pediatric ward, one of the first beds we passed was that of Anese Blanc, a three-year-old girl. When we presented the child with the box, she looked at us with a completely blank stare. At first, I wondered why Anese wasn't excited, then it slowly dawned on me that she had never received a gift in her life and had no idea what to do with it. Her mother then took the box and opened it up and showed her the toys and clothing inside. Slowly, Anese began to touch the toys and finally, showed a shy smile of happiness.

A volunteer reports:

> Seeing a small boy sitting alone with his unopened box, a member of our distribution team asked, "Why don't you open your box?" The boy answered, "My youngest sister is sick and could not come today. I am going to wait and give the gift to her so that we can open it together."

GERMANY

A Samaritan's Purse staff person reports:

> A non-Christian woman in Germany lost her job due to a mysterious ailment that took her voice. Since she had free time and loved children, she decided to host a collection center for Operation Christmas Child. She conducted all communication in writing with the central office in Germany as she trained and prepared for collection week. Shoeboxes streamed in, and on the last day of the collection, her doorbell rang. She opened the door to find a crowd of people carrying shoeboxes. Her heart filled with gratitude, and she wanted to greet the donors. Her voice returned and she asked the staff about their motivation for participating in Operation Christmas Child. She heard the Gospel message and gave her life that day to Jesus Christ.

UKRAINE

A nine-year-old boy writes:

> On Christmas Eve, I was hoping that I might receive a Christmas present, even though I knew that it probably wouldn't happen. I thought that I would pray about getting a gift, but realized that I did not even know who to pray to. This morning, Christmas morning, you came with gifts. The best thing was that you told me about the One I was praying to.

* * *

Millions of children—and the members of their families—throughout the world have learned to smile in the midst of difficulties because of strangers who, motivated by love, took time to fill shoeboxes. In fact, to me one of the most meaningful benefits of the program is the effect Operation Christmas Child has on those who give. What happens in the heart of the "giver" is amazing. During one of the deliveries in

Bosnia, among the gifts in his shoebox a boy found a baseball glove, a baseball, and an American flag. These gifts had been sent by a terminally ill boy in Ohio whose dying wish was that his favorite possessions be packed in a shoebox and sent to a boy in Bosnia.

Then there was a man who delivered shoeboxes from his church in Massachusetts to our collection center in Connecticut. One Christmas, Tim asked other volunteers to pray for him and his family as they felt God had laid a special burden on their hearts. While on a mission trip to Russia, Tim had the opportunity to distribute shoeboxes at an orphanage. There, Tim met a boy named Roman who had been born with no legs and only one arm. Tim's heart was broken with Christ's compassion at the sight of this boy. He simply fell in love with Roman.

The next Christmas, when Operation Christmas Child geared up, Tim arrived at the Connecticut distribution center. He had a very special helper in his truck—a six-year-old Russian boy named Roman. Tim proudly told our staff that Roman was now his son, and that if it had not been for Operation Christmas Child, he would never have had the chance to be a father to such a precious child.

Things like this happen when people give in the Name.

CHRISTMAS IN AFGHANISTAN

Because of the horrendous events of September 11, the 2001 Christmas season was particularly touching.

With a war raging in Afghanistan and the collapse of the Taliban government, once again enormous human needs surfaced in this land.

In addition to providing medical assistance, food, and shelter to Afghans moving by the thousands to refugee camps, Samaritan's Purse distributed 120,000 shoebox gifts to sites across Afghanistan. At each location, big smiles broke out as children looked wide-eyed through their boxes. Many parents were moved to tears as they saw their children's delight.

At the distribution in Dasht-i-Qala, the provincial governor explained that some of the gifts had come from New York children who had also suffered at the hands of terrorists and extremists. He acknowledged: "These gifts are from Christian children in the West," he said. "They want you to know that God has not forgotten you."

At one of the refugee camps where boxes were delivered, in the desolate plains of western Afghanistan, a tiny six-year-old girl named Bibi drew the attention of our workers.

If quiet, dark-eyed Bibi knew anything about the attacks on the United States by the Taliban and Al Qaeda, such understanding was well hidden behind her thoughtful eyes and tentative smile. What Bibi knew well was suffering. One day Bibi had been playing at a friend's house when an artillery shell hit her home and killed her parents and brother. With her family dead and nowhere to stay, the orphan began walking, and after two weeks ended up in a refugee camp.

Bibi was fed and given a place to sleep in a tent with another displaced family. Now at least she would not die of starvation or exposure as frigid winter weather gripped Afghanistan.

When a team from Samaritan's Purse arrived at the camp to distribute food, blankets, stoves, and shoes, Bibi asked one of the workers if she could have a pen and paper. Later she shyly handed a worker a small drawing that gave clues to her past life. The picture showed a child flying a kite while surrounded by tanks and missiles.

Not too many weeks later, Bibi was standing among hundreds of other children when several buses—raising large clouds of brown dust—rolled in. On each were hundreds of shoeboxes wrapped in bright Christmas paper. Some of these gifts were from New York City and had been personalized by a firefighter who had been at Ground Zero (site of the collapsed World Trade Center towers). This brave man, in spite of his own feelings of loss, wrote inside the boxes the names of every victim from the trade center and the Pentagon. Kirsten and Brielle Saracini also packed gifts to honor their father, a pilot with United Airlines, who died when his plane crashed into one of the Twin Towers.

Bibi, along with other children, had never seen such gifts, colorfully wrapped packages from strangers halfway around the world given in the Name of Jesus. All of this is possible because He set the standard as the most generous Giver of all. We contemplate what He gave on the cross—His life. But you see, Jesus gave His life every day in His Father's Name. Should we do any less?

> If anyone desires to come after Me, let him deny himself, and take up his cross daily, and follow Me.[2]

14

BY WHAT POWER— BY WHAT NAME?

Shortly after 9/11, President Bush announced that the perpetrators behind the evil attacks on our nation were Osama bin Laden and his Al Qaeda terrorist network. The president did not sit idle. He deployed troops and began an aggressive attack against the Taliban and Al Qaeda in Afghanistan, and threatened the same for any other nation harboring terrorists. Afghanistan had been under the control of a radical Islamic government that not only terrorized its own people, they even attacked America's shores.

I have been to Afghanistan and am aware of the difficulties that nation faces. Afghanistan has some of the worst living conditions anywhere on the face of the earth, including the highest child mortality rate. The average life expectancy is forty years. Due to the suffering of the Afghan people over the last twenty years, and the fall of the Taliban, I felt that we had an unprecedented opportunity to open a modern hospital in Afghanistan. There were several major obstacles, however. Could we get permission? Where would we build it? Could we recruit doctors? Would our staff be safe?

We dispatched a team to Afghanistan; they made their way into the northern part of the country into an area controlled by the Northern Alliance. The Afghan officials whom we met were excited about the idea and gave us permission to open a hospital in Kholm, a small village about thirty-five miles east of Mazar-e-Sharif.

The next obstacle: where to find doctors willing to go to such a remote and dangerous place. We prayed. Within a few months, God led us to physicians, some with past military experience, with a burden and love for the Afghan people. With so much political and social turmoil in the country, would our team be safe?

To answer this question, the local military commander disarmed the entire population, one of the first communities in all of Afghanistan to experience this. We have seen God open door after door. When we dedicated the opening of the hospital, more than five thousand Afghans came from all over the northern region to participate in the celebration. Everyone in the area knows that we are Christians. I believe this hospital will become a beacon of light and hope in a very dark corner of the Muslim world.

I am reminded that when Peter and John were healing the sick, the religious authorities questioned them:

> "By what power or by what name have you done this?" Then Peter, filled with the Holy Spirit, said to them, "Rulers of the people and elders of Israel: If we this day are judged for a good deed done to a helpless man . . . let it be known to you all . . . that by the name of Jesus Christ of Nazareth, whom you crucified, whom God raised from the dead, by Him this man stands here before you whole."[1]

Today in Afghanistan, we have committed medical doctors reaching out to patients who cannot pay for their medical services. These doctors could have lived a life of ease —yet they left their comfort zone for the discomforts of Afghanistan. Why? It is because of the Name of Jesus—that's what motivates them, that's what compels them, that's what drives them—to proclaim His great love.

I am reminded of the Apostle Peter, when he went into the temple and passed a lame beggar who asked for money. Peter replied, "Silver and gold I do not have, but what I do have I give you: In the name of Jesus Christ of Nazareth, rise up and walk."[2]

Throughout each generation, down through every century, this is what has motivated men and women to give their lives to go to the deepest darkest caverns of the world to shed the light of the Gospel. And when these lives are over, God will raise up other men and women to take their place, and the process will continue.

My grandfather, Dr. Nelson Bell, did the same—he left the comforts of his Virginia home in 1916 to serve in a hospital halfway around the world, in the interior of China, where he spent the early part of his adult life. He and my grandmother Virginia stayed until the Japanese invasion of China forced them to leave in 1941. I know that the soaring growth of the underground church today in China is a result of the faithfulness in sowing the seed of the Gospel by my grandparents, and so many others like them.

In 1923 my grandfather wrote a letter to a young American doctor who was considering joining his staff:

> The primary object of our work is to win souls to Jesus Christ. I am more and more convinced that we must stress this. You do not necessarily have to preach, but I would say that you must have the love for souls and desire to win them to the Master if you are to be a successful missionary.[3]

That says it all. The most important healing of all is the one that restores a human heart, sick from sin and shame, to wellness through reconciliation and love for God the Father.

My grandfather and others like him walked in the footsteps of the Great Physician—the Lord Jesus Christ.

His Name has always represented healing.

Some of the earliest accounts of Jesus' ministry included the healing of the sick. One of the first to benefit was Simon Peter's mother-in-law. Luke described what Jesus did:

> Now He arose from the synagogue and entered Simon's house. But Simon's wife's mother was sick with a high fever, and they made request of Him concerning her. So He stood over her and rebuked the fever, and it left her. And immediately she arose and served them.[4]

Why did Jesus heal people? I believe one reason was that He wanted to show His Father's heart toward mankind. God is gracious to His children.

"So the multitude marveled when they saw the mute speaking, the maimed made whole, the lame walking, and the blind seeing; and they glorified the God of Israel."[5] Jesus was pleased when people responded with thanksgiving to God and gave Him glory after seeing these miracles.

Certainly, the healing Jesus did added credibility to His claim to be the Son of God. The crowds swelled quickly when word got out that the carpenter's son from Nazareth had an awesome touch:

> And Jesus went about all Galilee, teaching in their synagogues, preaching the gospel of the kingdom, and healing all kinds of sickness and all kinds of disease among the people. Then His fame went throughout all Syria; and they brought to Him all sick people who were afflicted with various diseases and torments, and those who were demon-possessed, epileptics, and paralytics; and He healed them. Great multitudes followed Him—from Galilee, and from Decapolis, Jerusalem, Judea, and beyond the Jordan.[6]

Jesus is full of compassion. When people are sick, they will stop at nothing to find relief. In some of the countries where we work, people will travel hundreds of miles—sometimes days—to get to a missionary hospital. Why? Because it is their only hope for healing—there is no other choice. There are no other avenues available. When their physical needs have been met they are filled with love and gratitude.

In mission hospitals, patients often express a desire to know what has motivated the doctors and nurses to come and serve. The answer to this explains why missionary medicine has been such an effective tool for evangelism—medical missionaries have the opportunity to share their faith in Jesus Christ while ministering to the patients' physical needs. This gives people hope for a better life, and the Name of Jesus is advanced through time and across the vast reaches of the earth.

I am pleased to be associated with many dedicated medical personnel who work faithfully throughout the world to bring healing in the Name. At Samaritan's Purse we do this through our medical ministry, World Medical Mission.

THE GREAT PHYSICIAN

Jesus, the Great Physician, ministered to the sick by listening to them.

> Then it happened, as He was coming near Jericho, that a certain blind man sat by the road begging. And hearing a multitude passing by, he asked what it meant. So they told him that Jesus of Nazareth was passing by. And he cried out, saying, "Jesus, Son of David, have mercy on me!" Then those who went before warned him that he should be quiet; but he cried out all the more, "Son of David, have mercy on me!" So Jesus stood still and commanded him to be brought to Him. And when he had come near, He asked him, saying, "What do you want Me to do for you?" He said, "Lord, that I may receive my sight." Then Jesus said to him, "Receive your sight; your faith has made you well." And immediately he received his sight, and followed Him, glorifying God. And all the people, when they saw it, gave praise to God.[7]

Faith plays an important role in the healing process. This beggar called Jesus the Son of David, and cried out for the right thing, "Have mercy on me." He believed that Jesus could heal him—and Jesus did—and said, "Your faith has made you well."

> Now there is in Jerusalem by the Sheep Gate a pool, which is called in Hebrew, Bethesda, having five porches. In these lay a

> great multitude of sick people, blind, lame, paralyzed, waiting for the moving of the water . . . Now a certain man was there who had an infirmity thirty-eight years. When Jesus saw him lying there, and knew that he already had been in that condition a long time, He said to him, "Do you want to be made well?" The sick man answered Him, "Sir, I have no man to put me into the pool when the water is stirred up; but while I am coming, another steps down before me." Jesus said to him, "Rise, take up your bed and walk." And immediately the man was made well, took up his bed, and walked.[8]

Jesus showed compassion even to a man who did not know Him. This man had been looking into the water for healing power. But Jesus required that this man take his eyes off the pool and look at Him.

> And it happened when He was in a certain city, that behold, a man who was full of leprosy saw Jesus; and he fell on his face and implored Him, saying, "Lord, if You are willing, You can make me clean." Then He put out His hand and touched him, saying, "I am willing; be cleansed." Immediately the leprosy left him.[9]

Today there are many doctors serving in mission hospitals—as well as nurses and other medical personnel—who exhibit Christ's spirit of serving others, even in extremely difficult circumstances. They represent so well the Name of the Great Physician. Doctors who have served through World Medical Mission have shared with me some of their experiences.

HELENA'S HEALING

In the crude surroundings of a clinic under a portable canopy in Mozambique, one doctor and two nurses treated hundreds of patients in one day. Because of the lack of medical care in the country, neglected cases of malaria, diarrhea, fever, and anemia had attacked the population. Tropical heat and insects made conditions nearly unbearable. Garbled Portuguese translations complicated doctor-patient communication. When night fell, the medical team commuted back to home base in a sputtering boat.

Everything seemed extreme for the medical teams sent by Samaritan's Purse to help flood victims in Mozambique. Dr. Beth, a pediatrician and internist from Louisville, Kentucky, received a report of a girl with her intestines coming out. She assumed it was an exaggeration.

But it was true. An hour after the portable clinic had closed for the night, an eight-year-old girl named Helena was severely injured. While playing with her brother, the little boy swung her around, and the knife he wore on his belt accidentally stabbed her. The wound was relatively small, but about two feet of her intestine had threaded out.

Helena's family wrapped her as best they could and laid her in the bottom of a dugout canoe. Then her father paddled seven hours through the darkness against the swollen current of the Zambezi River. Her only hope, he knew, was in the hands of the doctor who had visited his village earlier that day. By the time he found the medical team it was past midnight, and Helena was in shock.

This team was not equipped for the complicated surgery Helena needed. Working by flashlight, they gave her IV fluids and antibiotics as they tried to stabilize her condition. Using a satellite phone, they arranged for a helicopter to evacuate her to the nearest hospital the next morning. Then Dr. Beth and nurse Natalie took turns through the night, comforting Helena and praying that she might survive. When they loaded her stretcher onto the helicopter, they didn't know if they would see her again.

Two weeks later Helena walked out of the hospital in Quelimane, her eyes shining brightly as she shyly showed a row of stitch marks across her tummy. Her surgery had been successful and infection avoided. Now she and her father were ready to go home to see her mother and family.

Before leaving, Helena's grateful father was curious and asked Dr. Beth why she and her staff would go to so much effort to help them out during this emergency. She told him that the reason they were in Mozambique was to reach out to those in need in the Name of the

Lord Jesus Christ. The fact that our medical team had just been in her village—and the village leaders knew their whereabouts—was not coincidental!

One day earlier, Helena's family would not have known that there were doctors nearby. One day later, the helicopter might not have been available. Everyone agreed that Helena's survival and recovery were a wonderful example of answered prayers and God's perfect timing.

This was Dr. Beth's second trip with World Medical Mission. Her team saw thousands of patients during five weeks in Mozambique, yet Helena is one that she will never forget. "If we accomplished nothing else the whole time," Dr. Beth later wrote, "it was all worth it."[10]

A BAPTISM IN ECUADOR

Like too many patients at missionary hospitals, the elderly woman from the rain forests of eastern Ecuador had waited too long before coming to see a doctor.

By the time she arrived at Hospital Vozandes-Shell, the woman was suffering from cervical cancer so advanced that her kidneys were shutting down. She had been unable to walk for two weeks. Even in the care of specialists at a state-of-the-art medical center, her case would have been considered hopeless. But at this mission hospital on the Amazon frontier, she found hope.

Dr. Mark, a surgeon from Greeneville, Tennessee, confirmed the grim diagnosis of the staff physician. Other than pain medication, there was little the hospital could do. Even prayer and counseling were problematic. The woman spoke only the obscure language of the Quichuas—descendants of the ancient Incas who are among the original settlers of eastern Ecuador.

To communicate with her, the hospital staff called for Lydia, a Quichuan Christian working in the hospital laundry. After Lydia shared the Gospel with her, the dying woman prayed to accept Jesus Christ as her personal Lord and Savior. Lydia then contacted the local Quichuan church, where the patient learned about baptism. She asked to be immersed the next Sunday.

Dr. Mark described the scene: "I was brought to tears standing at the side of the river as the sweet lady was carried on a stretcher into the river. A brief message was given in Spanish and then in Quichua, and then she was baptize—stretcher and all."

Recognizing the hope she had found in Jesus, the woman's daughter also accepted Christ. Rather than facing her death with despair, her family was able to share in her hope for eternal life.[11]

LIP SERVICE

Over the years, I have been blessed to know a host of wonderful medical missionaries. Some have gone on to heaven, but many are still serving the Lord on the foreign field today. A common thread they share is an incredible passion and persistence in overcoming all obstacles to advance the Name of Jesus through missionary medicine.

One of the most effective is Dr. Robert Foster. Not only has Bob been a medical pioneer as a surgeon in some of the roughest areas of Africa, he is also a superb Bible teacher and dynamic preacher of the Gospel.

On occasions while in Africa, I've traveled with Bob. Taking a trip with him is an adventure; no matter how tough a situation gets, he keeps smiling. Bob lives out what the Apostle Paul was teaching when he said, "Rejoice in all things."

Just like my Grandfather Bell, Bob is full of entertaining stories about his medical "adventures." One of my favorites is about the man who lost his lip.

Bob was at work one day when a truck arrived at the hospital clinic. In the back was a man named Kungarisi who was covered with blood.

"Can you fix Kungarisi's lip? My dog has just bitten it off," said Paul, the man who had brought the patient. Dr. Bob removed the rag tied around the lower half of the wounded man's face. Sure enough, about three-quarters of the bottom lip was gone. As they took Kungarisi into the operating room, Paul explained that his dog had been accidentally provoked when Kungarisi touched the animal's food.

"It would be so much easier to sew his lip back on rather than make a new lip," Bob explained to Paul. "Do you think you could find his lip?"

Paul agreed to go back to the scene of the accident and within a half hour he returned, gingerly holding the filthy piece of flesh rolled in a leaf between his finger and thumb. Bob had the orderly wash the lip in a saline solution while he explained to Kungarisi what he planned to do.

"I'm going to give you a little anesthetic. I can sew your lip back on."

The terrified patient shook his head. "I don't want any anesthetic."

"How am I going to sew this back on without giving you anesthetic?"

"No. No anesthetic. I'm afraid."

""There's nothing to be afraid of," Bob reassured him. But he knew that Africans were deathly afraid. They believed a person actually died and came to life again under anesthetic.

"You don't have to go to sleep for this," Bob explained. "I'll give you a local anesthetic and we can sew this in easily."

Kungarisi refused. After doing all he could to persuade him, Bob admitted defeat. He cleaned and dressed the wound as best he could.

When Kungarisi arrived home his wife looked at him in shock.

"What happened to you?" she cried.

He told her the whole story including Bob's offer to sew the lip back on. His wife was furious. "You go back there and get your lip sewed on. I don't want to live with a man without a lip!"

So, after lunch, Kungarisi turned up at the hospital and told Bob he was willing to have the surgery. Anticipating that Kungarisi might change his mind, Bob had left the sterilized lip in the saline solution on a stand in the operating room. Once more he and his assistant scrubbed up and were ready to proceed when Bob noticed a problem.

"Where's this guy's lip?" he shouted. "It's not here!"

The nurse was dumbfounded. "I don't know. We left it there before lunch." She checked with several nurses and then the cleaning man admitted that he'd thrown it out into the rubbish pile.

"Well, this fellow's come back here now and he wants his lip, so you go out and find it!" Bob ordered the man.

About ten minutes later, the cleaning man came in with the lip wrapped in the same gauze. Once more Bob cleaned it up, but now he was dubious about the outcome.

"I don't know if this will take after all this time and all this lip has been through," he warned Kungarisi. "But we'll try."

He sewed the lip back on. Bob really did not expect the operation to be a success.

When Kungarisi returned five days later to have the sutures removed, Bob couldn't believe his eyes. The lip had healed well enough so the man could use it, and in time he even got back full feeling.

About a month later, Kungarisi came back to thank Dr. Bob for what he had done for him. Bob reminded him, "You really shouldn't have a lip. This is a miracle. God's been good to you and you need to thank Him."

"How does a man thank God?" the huge African asked.

Bob explained that men in Scripture had asked that same question and he quoted from Psalm 116, "What shall I render unto the Lord for all of His goodness to me?"

"The man who wrote that many years ago said if we really want to thank God, the first thing we do is to take the salvation God offers us," Bob explained. As they continued speaking, Kungarisi's once-mangled lips broke into a smile of comprehension and before they had finished, his lips offered the sacrifice of praise.

From then on, he followed the Lord faithfully—offering Him far more than "lip service."[12]

MEDICINE ON THE MISSION FIELD

In the heart of Africa, a mother brought her frail three-year-old daughter to Tenwek Hospital, a mission hospital that has served the Kenyan people for many decades. She left carrying a much greater burden. Routine tests disclosed that the young girl was infected with the virus that causes Acquired Immunodefiency Syndrome, or AIDS. Further tests determined that the mother and father also were infected.

These tragedies are all too typical at missionary hospitals in eastern and southern Africa, where HIV (Human Immunodefiency Virus) and AIDS must be considered in every diagnosis. At Tenwek, more than half of the patients tested are HIV-positive. At Zambia's Zimba Hospital, the rate has topped 75 percent.

While there is no cure for AIDS, it does not mean that there is no hope. Tenwek and Zimba are among the hospitals staffed by Christian physicians who volunteer for short-term assignments through World Medical Mission. Compassion moves these doctors to give loving care and comfort to those dealing with the anguish and despair of AIDS. Faith enables them to tell patients facing death about the eternal life that Jesus Christ promises them. That's what happened with the family at Tenwek. They took the Gospel to heart and faced their remaining days with hope.

AIDS is not the only deadly sickness stalking the planet today. Millions of people in the world's poorest countries are dying from diseases that can be successfully treated. Each year, medical personnel serving with World Medical Mission help save countless lives while bearing witness to the Great Physician.

During 2001, we sent more than 300 doctors, dentists, and other medical personnel to 40 locations in 27 countries, including remote mission hospitals in places such as Bangladesh, Cameroon, Egypt, Ecuador, Papua New Guinea, Rwanda, and Togo. More than a dozen doctors served at the Samaritan's Purse hospital in southern Sudan. Other doctors were dispatched to help victims of flooding in Mozambique, earthquakes in El Salvador, and as I have mentioned, most recently, doctors have gone to Afghanistan to aid in treating the victims of war.

I thank God for physicians like Dr. Beth, Dr. Mark, Dr. Robert Foster, and a host of others who have gone to the dark corners of the earth in service to the Name that heals—the Great Physician.

15

THE NEW PLAGUE

When Jesus encountered people who wanted His healing touch, He never questioned them about how they became sick. The Bible says:

> And Jesus went about all Galilee, teaching in their synagogues, preaching the gospel of the kingdom, and healing all kinds of sickness and all kinds of disease among the people . . . And they brought to Him all sick people who were afflicted with various diseases and torments, and those who were demon-possessed, epileptics, and paralytics; and He healed them.[1]

Jesus was not condemning nor condescending. Why is that? We have to remember His mission. He came for the sick, not the healthy. He came for sinners, not the righteous. This was His mission. "Those who are well have no need of a physician, but those who are sick. I did not come to call the righteous, but sinners, to repentance."[2]

Many times organizations and businesses lose sight of their mission statement. You would be surprised how many people today do not even know the mission statement of the organization where they work, or the ministry in which they are involved. Jesus always had a clear focus and His mission was ever before Him: "to call sinners to repentance"—a very good lesson for you and me.

He used many different methods of healing, but He never prescreened individuals or sent them away because of previous sins. He dealt with the truth of their sins with love and mercy. He did not have to ask questions. He searched hearts and knew that all needed forgiveness and His healing touch. He forgave the woman caught in the act of adultery, which we read in the Scripture:

> Now early in the morning He came again into the temple, and all the people came to Him; and He sat down and taught them. Then the scribes and Pharisees brought to Him a woman caught in adultery. And when they had set her in the midst, they said to Him, "Teacher, this woman was caught in adultery, in the very act. Now Moses, in the law, commanded us that such should be stoned. But what do You say?" This they said, testing Him, that they might have something of which to accuse Him. But Jesus stooped down and wrote on the ground with His finger, as though He did not hear. So when they continued asking Him, He raised Himself up and said to them, "He who is without sin among you, let him throw a stone at her first." And again He stooped down and wrote on the ground. Then those who heard it, being convicted by their conscience, went out one by one, beginning with the oldest even to the last. And Jesus was left alone, and the woman standing in the midst. When Jesus had raised Himself up and saw no one but the woman, He said to her, "Woman, where are those accusers of yours? Has no one condemned you?" She said, "No one, Lord." And Jesus said to her, "Neither do I condemn you; go and sin no more."[3]

There is a pandemic of death and destruction loose in our world today that demands the same nonjudgmental response from those who serve others in the Name of Jesus. The pandemic that I speak of is Acquired

Immunodeficiency Syndrome, or AIDS, which is caused by the HIV (Human Immunodeficiency Virus). Millions are sick and dying without knowledge of the Son of the living God and the healing power that comes through His Name. Tens of millions will become ill and die in the years to come. It is a plague like those visited upon Egypt during the days of Moses in the Jewish captivity. The World Health Organization has called it "the most devastating disease humankind has ever faced."[4] The virus that causes AIDS has no known cure, no preventive vaccine, nor any hope of successful treatment in the near future. There are expensive drugs that can prolong life for a while, but for the most part, these can be afforded only by the wealthy. Still, they are not a cure.

When AIDS first came onto the world scene, many wanted to stigmatize it as a homosexual problem, saying, "They are just getting what they deserve." For various reasons, most Christians—including myself—wanted to stay as far away from the issue as possible.

It is true that sinful behavior by homosexuals is a major factor in the spread of this deadly plague. But it is also true that in Africa, India, the Caribbean, and many other parts of the world, including the United States, HIV/AIDS is also caused by sinful heterosexual behavior, which threatens to annihilate men, women, and—sadly—children of an entire generation.

To many, Christians think of AIDS as a sinner's disease. No question, there are consequences to our actions, and we have to take responsibility for the choices we make in life.

As a pilot, if I fly at forty-one thousand feet and stick my head out the window of a pressurized airplane, I will not be able to survive more than just a few minutes, if that long. Why? Because I am outside the boundaries that God created for me to live a healthy life. I like to scuba dive (though I'm not very good at it). But if I stick my head just an inch under the water without a breathing apparatus, I will not last more than a few minutes, if that long. Why? Because I am outside the boundaries God created.

Likewise, when sex is experienced outside the boundaries God established—which is the marriage relationship between husband and wife—it threatens our health and even our very life. Why?

Because we are engaging in behavior that is outside the boundaries God designed for us.

The church of Jesus Christ has a tremendous opportunity to reach out to those living with AIDS. Little has been said to those who are without hope of cure—those who are already infected and living with AIDS. Too often we have just looked the other way. I believe strongly that the way the church chooses to respond to HIV/AIDS, which is both a moral and a health crisis, will define how seriously our generation takes the Great Commission.

In past generations, Christians responded to the Great Commission by going to China to preach the Gospel, as my grandfather did. Other generations went to the jungles of Southeast Asia and Africa. Every generation seems to encounter some challenge that tests its resolve. Brave Christian servants like David Livingstone in Africa, and William Wilberforce in England, rallied the church to fight slavery and help break the chains of the oppressed. Over the next twenty years, one of the great mission fields for our generation will be to reach out to the 100 million people who will be infected with HIV and possibly die without ever hearing the Gospel of Jesus Christ.

This topic is difficult to discuss, which is why it is often ignored. But Jesus never shied away from tough issues. His ministry encompassed disagreement and conflicts. I believe that if He were physically present on earth today, He would be reaching out to those engulfed by this disease. He would show love and compassion, and would use His healing power in order to draw men, women, and children to Himself, even in the face of HIV/AIDS. Now throughout the world, millions are dying alone, rejected, hopeless—captives of a hideous sickness. Just how will we respond?

BACKGROUND OF A CRISIS

When I first became aware of HIV/AIDS during the 1980s, I was appalled. The Bible pulls no punches in labeling sin. Sin is sin. God's response to wickedness is without prejudice. Every sinner, regardless of the sins committed, needs redemption found in the cross of Christ.

Jesus came to save sinners, not to condemn them. The Bible says: "For God did not send His Son into the world to condemn the world, but that the world through Him might be saved."[5] Jesus ate with sinners, He talked with them, and He visited with them in their homes. This was one of the chief complaints of the religious leaders of that day. He associated with sinners; they did not. You see, Jesus' mission statement was always in clear focus.

Because of the ministry at Samaritan's Purse, my first real insight into understanding this pandemic was through missionary hospitals in other countries. Our ministry has watched this plague unfold before our eyes, primarily in Africa. Since the late 1970s, we have been sending doctors and nurses to clinics and hospitals in Africa. When the disease which became known as AIDS was first identified in the early 1980s, we asked personnel in these missionary hospitals, "Have you seen any AIDS patients?" the answer was "No." But it wasn't long until reports trickled in that a few people were showing up as HIV-positive. Five years later, the number of hospital beds occupied by patients suffering with AIDS had increased to 10 to 20 percent of the hospital's total bed count. In some locations in Africa, 50 percent or more of the patients in hospitals now suffer with AIDS or AIDS-related diseases.

Unfortunately, when those sick with AIDS come to missionary hospitals there is little to do for them in terms of medicine because there is no cure, and no hope of a cure. We make them as comfortable as possible and help them die with dignity. In the process, we have the opportunity to point them to eternal life. Every person has a soul, and the greatest thing that we can do is to share with each and every one the hope that we have in Jesus Christ, the Savior of our souls.

Why is HIV/AIDS spreading so rapidly in Third World nations?

The answer is a tangle of moral, social, physical, economic, and environmental factors. Of significant embarrassment to me is that American culture and mass media contribute to a sexually promiscuous mind-set that aggressively promotes alternative lifestyles that are against God's commands. I believe this has accelerated the spread of HIV.

For decades American TV and movies have been popular in other nations. The story lines in our entertainment have increasingly glorified sexual activity of all types outside of marriage. In most television entertainment, some type of extramarital sexual contact is suggested, endorsed, or depicted. Hollywood portrays fornication and adultery as attractive and glamorous. The people who do these things appear to get by without negative consequences; everyone looks happy, and physical lust reigns.

This scenario does not reflect reality, of course. Much of the world, however, looks up to America and the West because of material, political, scientific, and military achievements, and the freedoms we enjoy. They want to emulate the Western lifestyle that they have seen portrayed on television, where promiscuity is prevalent.

There are other causes, of course. In Africa, like so many other parts of the world, more jobs are available in the large cities. For many families in rural villages, a man must leave his wife and children and go far away to the city. Because of the cost and difficulty of transportation, he may be gone for many months or even years. While away, he may get involved with prostitutes—the city slums are full of brothels populated by impoverished women who have also fled to the city to survive. With few alternatives available, these women turn to one of the oldest trades in the world—that is, to sell themselves—often for pennies. It is an evil cycle that leads to despair and the proliferation of sin that can end in death.

The statistics on the HIV/AIDS crisis are alarming:

- In 2001, three million people died of AIDS.
- Worldwide AIDS is the fourth leading cause of death.[6]
- An estimated 28,000,000 people have already died of AIDS.[7] Of these, 70 percent lived in sub-Saharan Africa.[8] In this region there are more than 13.5 million AIDS orphans.[9]
- About thirteen million children have lost one or both parents to AIDS.
- In seven African countries, more than 20 percent of the 15–49 age-group is infected with HIV.[10]

- In the small African nation of Swaziland, 32 percent of the population is infected with HIV, and there are forty thousand AIDS orphans.[11]
- The majority of the AIDS patients in South Africa are ages 15–30.[12] Some communities in Africa have lost their entire population from age twenty through the mid-forties.
- Every 10 seconds, someone in the world is infected with the HIV virus,[13] and there are 5 million new HIV-infected persons each year. Worldwide, approximately 40 million people are infected with HIV (some say this a very conservative number)
- India and the Caribbean regions are now reporting the highest rates of increase in HIV infections.
- Every day 1,800 babies are born infected with HIV. Worldwide, 2.7 million children are infected. Each month, 50 thousand boys and girls die of AIDS.

Of the forty million people who are infected worldwide, many have become HIV-positive because of their own sinful behavior. Representing the greatest tragedy in this new plague are the innocent victims of this deadly disease who have become infected through the sinful behavior of others, often by loved ones who engaged in promiscuous sex, extramarital affairs, homosexual relationships, prostitution, or intravenous drug use, and then transmitted the virus to them. A small percentage have been infected through transfusions of contaminated blood or they were born HIV-positive because their mothers were infected.

In Western nations like the United States, those who are HIV positive have access to some medications that control or slow down the virus. But there is no cure or any hope for a successful vaccine in the foreseeable future. The question for Christians is the same as the question that appears on the popular WWJD bracelets worn today—"What Would Jesus Do?"

One thing I know for sure: He would not turn His back. Jesus would use His power as the Son of God to heal bodies, minds, and hearts.

So what can we do? With no cure for HIV/AIDS available, some type of alternative plan is needed because of the grim outlook. Here's a scenario built on valid assumptions: Some researchers report that a vaccine, which will be effective in offering protection against AIDS, may be ten or more years away. With the current rate at which the number of people infected with HIV is escalating, it is estimated that the number of people who are infected may reach fifty million over the next ten years. Added to the forty million who are already infected, that means close to one hundred million people will be HIV-positive by 2012! The estimated death toll for 2001, due to AIDS, was three million. That's three million lost lives. It is reasonable to assume the death toll will rise each year. Even assuming that no increase occurs, and present numbers stay the same, thirty million or more people can be expected to die of AIDS during the next decade. All are souls for whom Christ died and shed His blood on Calvary's cross.

We must do something on behalf of the Name.

A BATTLE STRATEGY

Although this virus and disease have no cure now, I do think the epidemic can be contained. It won't happen in one or two years, but through biblically based education, lifestyle changes, and certainly by proclaiming the Gospel, broken lives can be transformed and the tide turned.

In February of 2002, Samaritan's Purse hosted an international HIV/AIDS conference in Washington, D.C., called Prescription for Hope. Our ministry thought it was of absolute importance to assemble Christian workers who are on the front line in fighting this disease around the world. We also wanted to show how some in the church are already involved in this battle. But the role of the church needs to increase. So far, the homosexual community and the United Nations have had the loudest voices on the issue. The church has an unprecedented opportunity to take the love of Jesus Christ and the hope that is found in Him to millions who may never otherwise hear how God can change their lives. True, government agencies have not always invited the church to the table to share their views, but perhaps this can change as the church becomes more involved in reaching out to those who are facing this horrible epidemic. It's important to note, however, that in hospitals, clinics, and dispensaries around the world, Christian missionaries and national workers have quietly been on the forefront of treating HIV/AIDS victims, as well as aiding orphans and providing hospice care.

The conference convened with nearly one thousand in attendance from eighty-six countries, including physicians, missionary AIDS workers, church leaders, representatives of humanitarian foundations and compassionate care ministries, and government officials. About one-third of those present were "frontline" providers of care to HIV/AIDS patients.

As a result of this conference and our previous experience, I would like to suggest several components of a strategy that I believe needs to be mounted on behalf of the church in an effort to combat HIV/AIDS:

Leadership

The church should be leading, not following or watching this fight. Let's stop waiting for the government or the medical or scientific industry to solve this problem. Let's put this issue at the top of our agendas as individuals, churches, denominations, and Christian organizations.

A *Time* magazine cover story dated February 12, 2001, stated:

> Without treatment, those with HIV will sicken and die; without prevention, the spread of infection cannot be checked. South Africa has no other means available to break the vicious cycle except to change everyone's sexual behavior—and that is not happening. The essential missing ingredient is leadership. Neither the countries of the region nor those of the wealthy world have been able or willing to provide it.[14]

The church must help meet the leadership deficit not only in South Africa but also in the rest of the world.

The church must stop the finger-pointing and condemnation. "See, we told you so," is not going to cut it. This is about as effective as yelling "baby killers" at young girls going into abortion clinics. That will not change a girl's heart. But if we reach out in love and compassion to individuals with HIV/AIDS, we can try to win them to faith in Jesus Christ. Everyone needs forgiveness and cleansing from unrighteousness and the hope of eternal life in heaven.

Jesus came to rescue sinners. People infected with HIV/AIDS are sinners, the same as you and me.

Education

An education effort developed in Uganda has been a key in lowering the HIV infection rate from around 30 percent to less than 10 percent in that country. Their curriculum was developed by a missionary and was mandated by Uganda's president to be taught in every school. This Bible-based approach should be duplicated elsewhere.

Education requires telling the truth concerning improper sexual behavior and how HIV and other diseases can be transmitted through it. It is shocking to learn how many millions still do not know the most basic information about how HIV is transmitted and how it can be prevented. Knowledge is power. The more men and women know, the more control they will have over their lives. It does not necessarily mean that just because people "know," they will not engage in risky behavior; some people will continue to live questionable lifestyles in spite of all the warnings.

Men and women must be educated about the risk associated with lifestyles and behavior that are outside of God's boundaries. Pastors everywhere should include in their preaching and teaching sexual abstinence before marriage and faithfulness to one's husband or wife in marriage, as the Bible teaches: "Since there is so much immorality, each man should have his own wife, and each woman her own husband."[15]

As I have carefully read the literature concerning HIV/AIDS, it has become very obvious to me that condoms are not the answer. There are scientific reports that show condoms, if properly used, may offer some degree of protection against HIV and other sexually transmitted diseases, but distribution of condoms encourages promiscuous sexual behavior. For the last ten years, the United Nations and world health organizations, along with the United States government, have distributed hundreds of millions of condoms. In spite of this mass distribution, the HIV/AIDS infection rate has continued to climb. *The only answer for reversing the tide is to adopt God's standards for sexual behavior: abstinence before marriage and faithfulness to one's spouse, of the opposite sex, in marriage.*

Allocation of Resources

Where possible, the church needs to work with governments and other agencies around the world to help them allocate resources to education and programs that are worthwhile. I am thankful that the United States government contributes one-third of the aid for the fight against HIV/AIDS worldwide.[16] It is only fitting that we do this since our declining moral values, found in our popular music, movies, and television programming, are a contributing cause to the spread of HIV.

Present Clearly the Hope That We Have in Jesus Christ

I am not naive about human nature. HIV/AIDS is getting a great deal of attention because there is no cure and it leads to certain death, but there are a number of other sexually transmitted diseases. Some have no cure. Some can be treated, but researchers report that resistance to current medications is occurring. All sexually transmitted diseases can lead to pain and suffering. These can devastate health and, in some instances, cause death. No matter how much we educate, sin will still deceive, and people will still engage in life-threatening, high-risk behavior to get a moment of sexual gratification. But isn't it possible to make a dent? If we can reduce the annual infection rate by just 20 percent through biblically based education, that would prevent the infection of one million people each year, or 40 percent—two million people—all souls of utmost importance to God. There is not a cure for HIV/AIDS. But there is hope if we turn to God and follow His laws and commands. This battle can be won in time and with His help. It can be done.

Followers of Jesus Christ should reach out in love to those who do not have the same hope that we have in Christ Jesus. "Love suffers long and is kind . . . bears all things, believes all things, hopes all things, endures all things. Love never fails."[17] Let's reach out in ways in which we have never reached out before and demonstrate with actions—and not just words—that we care for others because God cares. Every soul is precious in the sight of God. Shouldn't every soul be precious in our sight?

THE CALL TO BATTLE

My desire is to see an army of Christian men and women going out across the globe to wage war against HIV/AIDS. Ultimately, every army is only as strong as its soldiers. The army of the Lord Jesus Christ is no different. I want to tell just one story of an individual "foot soldier" in the war against HIV/AIDS.

I first met this Canadian ball of energy, Avis Rideout, at the Prescription for Hope conference. Avis has a passion to see both babies with AIDS and sinners find new life.

When Avis and her husband, Roy, went to Thailand as missionaries in 1972, neither of them ever imagined they would someday be frontline soldiers, battling a horrible disease. Avis was a nurse, but at that time HIV/AIDS had not even appeared as a health issue. Thailand, long known for its sexual promiscuity, soon became one of Asia's most infected countries.

In the mid-1990s Avis's understanding of God's intentions for her life were radically altered during a visit to a government-sponsored hospital ward for babies who were HIV-positive. While there, Avis saw babies, sick and dying because of the actions of others, lying on their mats, some with swollen stomachs and covered with sores—all untouched and alone. Because of fear, believing that even the slightest contact with the sick infants might put them at risk of contracting HIV, caregivers wore rubber gloves and kept as far away as they could from these tiny ones who had no one to love them.

"I saw that these babies were dying, not from HIV, but from rejection," Avis says. Her heart broke.

She and Roy saw a baby girl named Nikki. She had lost her hair and was "skin and bones" and about to die. Moved by the compassion of Christ, they decided to take her home. Not long after, the Rideouts opened the Agape Home, a place devoted solely to the care of HIV infants.

Since then, 129 HIV babies have arrived at Agape Home where each one is held, touched, kissed, and loved. Avis says, "It's about giving quality life, and hope when there is no hope. We have seen fantastic results, because we are able to bring them in and love and care for them . . . through touching, holding, and talking to them."

Each child receives medical and nutritional care. But best of all each one is given a tender, personal touch and love in the Name of Jesus. And no child ever dies alone. Members of the staff hold the dying infant, expressing affection softly, and singing of the love of Jesus, repeating verses of comfort from Scripture. Some of these children, like Nikki, have grown and are strong. Many would appear to be normal children. In Nikki's case, she is still HIV-positive. Someday she will die, but if it were not for Avis and Roy, Nikki and 129 others would have been discarded with no hope. Each child that comes into this home is given something he or she desperately needs, and that is love: the love of Christ that flows through those who carry His Name. Jesus says, "Inasmuch as you did it to one of the least of these My brethren, you did it to Me."[18]

At the Prescription for Hope conference, Avis made clear that there is a disease more deadly than AIDS. "I am an evangelist," she said. "My heart throbs constantly for the lost souls of this world. I see in America, and other countries around the world, a greater disease than AIDS—it is sin . . . Sin is death. But there is eternal hope and peace through Jesus Christ . . . If there had been just one AIDS baby dying without hope, God would have sent His Son to save that one child."

Avis is so right. By ministering to the millions—young and old—we can go on a rescue mission to save those infected with AIDS and those blinded by sin by sharing with them God's grace, mercy, and forgiveness found only through the Name.

16

THE BLOOD OF THE LAND

Again the blood flows in this ancient land.

As the final pages of this book are written the headlines scream for peace. The Bible speaks of "'peace, peace!' when there is no peace."[1]

A recent issue of a newsmagazine displayed the pictures of two teenage girls, Rachel and Ayat. Rachel, an Israeli, went to the market in southern Jerusalem to buy groceries for the Passover celebration. Ayat, a Palestinian, went to the same store to purchase revenge for centuries of hate. At the very moment the two girls met at the entrance, Ayat, the suicide bomber, detonated the explosives strapped to her body. Both girls died. Two young precious lives were snuffed out.[2]

Why such senseless violence? What is it about this "not so holy" Holy Land that has inflamed passions for centuries? Although the terrain and climate are surprisingly varied for such a small country, the land is not abundantly rich in natural resources. The borders, even when stretched, cover but ten thousand square miles—one-sixteenth the size of California. The population of Israel is five and a half million, about the number of residents who live in the greater Philadelphia or Toronto area. So what's the big deal?

It is the Lord Himself who said: "This is Jerusalem; I have set her in the midst of the nations and the countries around her."[3]

Jerusalem is the center of the earth geographically. In the Church of the Holy Sepulcher they have a mark on the floor, equidistant between the place of the cross and the sepulcher. This is called "the center of the world." North, in the Bible, is north of Jerusalem, East is east of Jerusalem, South is south of Jerusalem, and West is west of Jerusalem. One has only to take a glance at a relief map to see that Jerusalem is located on a land bridge that touches Asia, Africa, and Europe.

Jerusalem is also the salvation center of the earth spiritually. At Jacob's well, the Lord Jesus told the woman from Sychar that "salvation is of the Jews." He was speaking of man's greatest need. To be sure, man is hungry and needs to be fed. He is naked and needs to be clothed. He is illiterate and needs to be educated. But man is lost and needs to be saved. And God alone is the Savior. "And there is no other God besides Me, a just God and a Savior . . . Look to Me, and be saved, all you ends of the earth! For I am God, and there is no other."[4] The only salvation that God ever provided for the world was outside the gates of Jerusalem, a place called Mount Calvary.

Jerusalem is also the storm center of the world prophetically. Statesmen and world leaders have always been aware that Jerusalem is the tinderbox. As we look into the near and distant future, troubles in Asia, Europe, and Africa are minuscule compared to the volatile eruptions in the Middle East as it relates to the city of Jerusalem.

God said: "Behold, I will make Jerusalem a cup of drunkenness to all the surrounding peoples, when they lay siege against Judah and Jerusalem. And it shall happen in that day, that I will make Jerusalem a very heavy stone for all peoples . . . though all nations of the earth are gathered against it."[5]

Jerusalem shall be the glory center of the world ultimately! Almighty God has purposed that this earth shall be reconciled to Him. The Lord's house shall be established in the top of the mountains.[6] All nations shall flow unto it. The God of Jacob will teach the nations of

His ways. Men, all men, will walk in His paths. The law shall go forth from Zion, and the word of the Lord from Jerusalem. Nation shall not lift up sword against nation; neither shall they learn war anymore. [7]

We do know that by God's choosing, the land of Israel is where He determined the pivotal struggles of human history would occur. In fact, this ground has soaked up more blood from every generation than any other place on earth, from the time God gave His covenant to Abraham to this very day. This same ground absorbed the most precious blood of all, the life-giving flow that ran down a Roman cross where the Lord Jesus Christ was lifted up and died for the sins of this world.

I have traveled extensively throughout the Middle East. Countless times I have crossed from Jordan to Israel by way of the Allenby Bridge, which spans the Jordan River even to this day. This bridge was built to honor General Allenby, the Commander of the British Forces, whom God used so miraculously to make conquest of Jerusalem without firing a single shot. I have many friends in the region and have worked there for years. It is an intriguing part of the world. Divisions run so deep that any solution seems impossible.

Library shelves sag with books trying to explain the dilemma of the Middle East. Any night of the week, you can find pundits debating possible solutions to the Arab-Israeli problem. Diplomats from every American administration since World War II have made countless trips to further "the peace process." How in the world did such a thorny mess develop?

I know of only one place to look for sure insight and hope. Let's go back to the Scriptures. In the following pages, I want to give you a thumbnail sketch, beginning with God's covenant with Abraham and the major passages that reaffirm this covenant and the prophecies about the State of Israel. It all started with a promise.

A LAND PROMISED

To Abraham and his descendants God promised a land. Abraham, or Abram as he was then known, was living nearly a thousand miles away in Ur of the Chaldeans, which is present-day Iraq.

> Now the LORD had said to Abram: "Get out of your country, from your family and from your father's house, to a land that I will show you. I will make you a great nation; I will bless you and make your name great; and you shall be a blessing. I will bless those who bless you, and I will curse him who curses you; and in you all the families of the earth shall be blessed."
>
> So Abram departed as the LORD had spoken to him, and Lot went with him . . . So they came to the land of Canaan . . . Then the LORD appeared to Abram and said, "To your descendants I will give this land."[8]

Because of Abraham and Sarah's unbelief, they decided to give God some help. They took matters into their own hands, instead of waiting on the Lord.

Aren't we all prone to that? It was Sarah's "brilliant" idea (let the record show that Abraham voiced no objection) to help God along by arranging for Abraham to have a child with the maid Hagar. A boy named Ishmael was the result.

Not until fourteen years later did Abraham and Sarah have the son that God promised them. His name was Isaac. Still, Ishmael did not fade into obscurity. After Hagar bore Ishmael, God told her, "Arise, lift up the lad and hold him with your hand, for I will make him a great nation."[9] In time, Ishmael became the father of twelve princes who had many descendants that roamed the deserts of northern Arabia as nomads. Modern-day Arabs trace their forebears to Ishmael.[10]

Sadly, the blood spilled on the soil of this land is a result of Sarah and Abraham's impatience and disbelief. The results are seen even to this day. When Ayat the suicide bomber killed Rachel in the Jerusalem market, it was a descendant of Ishmael coming against a descendant of Isaac—cousin killing cousin.

God's covenant was through Isaac. Why? Because Isaac was the son that God promised to Abraham and Sarah. Ishmael was not the promised son. Isaac's son, Jacob, had twelve sons who populated the land. In time, a famine drove his descendants to Egypt as immigrants where they lived for four centuries. God, then, reaffirmed to Moses that the covenant for the land still stood: "And I will bring you into the land which I swore to give to Abraham, Isaac, and Jacob; and I will give it to you as a heritage: I am the LORD."[11]

A LAND OCCUPIED

This familiar story never grows old. God chose Moses to lead His people, the children of Israel, out of Egyptian captivity back to the land promised to Abraham through his son Isaac. After the miraculous escape across the Red Sea and the drowning of the Egyptian army, the Israelites were poised to take up residence in Canaan. Because of their unbelief and disobedience, this entire generation—consisting of perhaps several million people—wandered for forty years in the desert. Eventually, through the leadership of Joshua, Moses' successor, the Israelites entered their promised homeland—"flowing with milk and honey."

Long before the Jews ever made it to Canaan, though, God told Moses:

> Behold, you will rest with your fathers; and this people will rise and play the harlot with the gods of the foreigners of the land, where they go to be among them . . . When I have brought them to the land flowing with milk and honey, of which I swore to their fathers, and they have eaten and filled themselves and grown fat, then they will turn to other gods and serve them; and they will provoke Me and break My covenant.[12]

Sure enough, that is exactly what happened. Just as God had foretold:

> I led you up from Egypt and brought you to the land of which I swore to your fathers; and I said, "I will never break My covenant with you. And you shall make no covenant with the inhabitants of this land; you shall tear down their altars." But you have not obeyed My voice. Why have you done this? Therefore I also said, "I will not drive them out before you; but they shall be thorns in your side, and their gods shall be a snare to you."[13]

Those "thorns" still prick the Jews to this day—often drawing perfect blood—and Israel has no lasting peace.

In time, the Jews demanded a king. It was not God's perfect plan, but He gave them their request in one named Saul.[14] When Saul forsook the Lord, God raised up the shepherd boy David to tend His very own flock—the people of Israel. Under the reigns of King David and his son and successor, Solomon, Israel reached the peak of its ancient glory. This kingdom encompassed much of present-day Israel, Lebanon, and parts of Jordan and Syria.

EXODUS IN REVERSE

After centuries of continual disobedience, in the year 586 B.C., God finally said, "Enough!" God sent judgment on Israel for their sins, and allowed the Babylonians to capture Jerusalem. Many Jews were carried off to Babylon as slaves, while only a remnant remained in Israel under the rule of others. The psalmist wrote,

> You have given us up like sheep intended for food, and have scattered us among the nations.[15]

> By the rivers of Babylon we sat and wept when we remembered Zion.[16]

Through the prophet Ezekiel, God stated His reasons:

> Moreover the word of the LORD came to me, saying: "Son of man, when the house of Israel dwelt in their own land, they defiled it by their own ways and deeds . . . Therefore I poured out My fury on them for the blood they had shed on the land, and for their idols with which they had defiled it. So I scattered them among the nations, and they were dispersed throughout the countries; I judged them according to their ways and their deeds. When they came to the nations, wherever they went, they profaned My holy name."[17]

Under the leadership of prophet Nehemiah, a number of the captives from Babylon eventually returned and rebuilt the wall around Jerusalem. In time, the Jews repented, but the land was no longer theirs. For the next six hundred years, the Jews chafed under a succession of foreign rulers.

When Jesus began His public ministry at thirty years of age, many people of that day were looking to Him to emerge as the political messiah—the one who would restore the kingdom of Israel and drive the Romans out of their land. To our knowledge, Jesus visited Jerusalem only seven times. When He made His last visit—His triumphal entry into Jerusalem—as a humble servant on a donkey rather than a conquering military hero, He actually predicted more hard times for the city and the people that He loved:

> Now as He drew near, He saw the city and wept over it, saying, "If you had known, even you, especially in this your day, the things that make for your peace! But now they are hidden from your eyes. For days will come upon you when your enemies will build an embankment around you, surround you and close you in on every side, and level you, and your children within you, to the ground; and they will not leave in you one stone upon another, because you did not know the time of your visitation."[18]

A DESPERATE STAND FOR FREEDOM

After Christ died on the cross, was buried, then rose from the grave and returned to heaven, the Jews made one last, all-out attempt to throw off Roman rule and reclaim their nation. This resistance climaxed in A.D. 70 when a huge contingent of the Roman army surrounded Jerusalem and laid siege to the city—ironically during Passover.

The citizens of Jerusalem fought fiercely, but slowly the Romans wore the Jews down. Supplies inside the city ran low, and with almost no food left, "famished citizens gnawed leather sandals and killed their fellows for a piece of bread."[19] At night, the more daring residents would sneak outside the city walls to rummage for food. If caught by the Roman soldiers, they would be crucified. When a Jewish soldier was captured, the Romans cut off his hands and sent him back inside the city walls. The Romans reasoned that the man could not fight but he would have to eat—thereby increasing demand on an already scant food supply.[20]

The historian Josephus wrote:

> The famine, devoured the people by whole houses and families; the upper rooms were full of women and children that were dying by famine; and the lanes of the city were full of the dead bodies of the aged; the children also and the young men wandered about the marketplaces like shadows, all swelled with the famine, and fell down dead wheresoever their misery seized them . . . Nor was there any lamentation made under these calamities, nor were heard any mournful complaints; . . . for those who were just going to die, looked upon those that were gone to their rest before them with dry eyes and open mouths. A deep silence also, a kind of deadly night, had seized upon the city.[21]

As the siege continued, the Romans methodically destroyed the entire city.

With the temple aflame, the Roman commander, Titus, went in for a look. Josephus reports: "They [the Jews] were everywhere slain, and everywhere beaten. And as for a great part of the people, they were weak and without arms, and had their throats cut wherever they were caught. Now, round about the altar lay dead bodies heaped upon one another; as at the steps going up to it ran a quantity of their blood."[22]

Jerusalem finally fell, and those captured were executed or sent off into slavery.[23] The city, in total ruin, was abandoned. The Jews would not rule or have significant influence there for twenty centuries.

In spite of this, does it mean that God's promise was broken? No! A promise is a promise. His covenant stands forever. The promise of God given four thousand years ago is in effect today; it will be in effect tomorrow and ten thousand years from now. God always keeps His word. His Word cannot be overturned by the United Nations, by the will of politicians—by anyone. A few years ago an Israeli leader, when asked to give some of their land in exchange for peace, was reported to have said, "We cannot give to others what God has promised to us."

THE HOMELESS CENTURIES

A remnant of the Jews remained in the land, but the Romans continued to rule with an iron fist for another two hundred–plus years during which they rebuilt Jerusalem and erected a pagan shrine on the foundations of the temple. In A.D. 611, Jerusalem was destroyed, once again, by the invading Persians.

To further understand the tensions in Jerusalem today, it is important to know about the founder of Islam, Muhammad. He claimed to have risen from the temple site in Jerusalem and to have spoken with the angel Gabriel. This legend about Muhammad's experience turned Jerusalem into a holy site for Muslims. Significantly, this same spot is where Jews believe Abraham went to sacrifice Isaac centuries before.[24]

After Muhammad's death in 632, an army of Arabs—descendants of Ishmael—sympathetic to him and his creed, conquered the land God had promised to Abraham and his descendants through Isaac. Later the Muslims built a mosque, known today as the Dome of the Rock, on top of the very foundations where Solomon's temple had once stood.

The followers of Muhammad ruled the area for more than four hundred years until Jerusalem was wrenched from them in 1099, during the infamous Crusades. Sporadic warfare continued until in a *jihad* or holy war, the Muslims conquered Jerusalem again in 1187.

Many more centuries passed as control of the city was juggled back and forth, with power held for long periods by the Mamluks of Egypt and the Ottoman Turks.

It wasn't until the late 1800s that the push for resettlement, fueled by the Zionist movement, gained momentum. The Zionist movement originally worked for the establishment of a Jewish community in Palestine, and later supported a modern State of Israel. Persecution of the Jews in Russia spurred these efforts. A magnetic Jew named Theodor Herzl led the Zionist movement. His work was continued and later expanded by Dr. Chaim Weizmann. Under their leadership, the Zionist movement began purchasing tens of thousands of acres of land in a determined effort to once again claim their home. Around 1914, the number of Jewish residents in the area—then known as Palestine—numbered more than one hundred thousand.[25]

For over two thousand years, Israel had been only a nation in history that did not exist geographically. The Jewish people were scattered throughout the nations of the world. Their language ceased to be officially spoken anywhere in the world and was considered by most to be a dead and forgotten language, used and studied mainly by scholars—much like Latin.

When my father was growing up on a farm in Charlotte, North Carolina, he read the biblical prophecies about the State of Israel, which were a mystery. At that time, Israel did not exist! How could this be? Yet, the Bible spoke of Israel in the last days.

Unbeknownst to him and most people at that time, God was fulfilling one of His great prophecies. He was beginning to move His people back to their land. The slow rebirth of their Hebrew language was beginning, and is spoken in Israel today. Again, God keeps His promises!

Near the end of World War I, the British captured Palestine, or what is now modern Israel, as part of an allied offensive against Germany and the Ottoman Empire. In November of 1917, the British issued the Balfour Declaration, which stated that Great Britain favored the establishment in Palestine of a "national home for the Jewish people."

When the Allies won the war, Palestine came under British military administration, and Jewish immigration to unoccupied territory or "wastelands" was encouraged. Soon areas of the land promised to the Jew, which had been uninhabited and uncultivated for vast periods of time, were reclaimed. The Arabs who had controlled the region for more than a thousand years objected to the influx of new Jewish neighbors. Fighting broke out periodically—more bloodshed on both sides.

In the decades before World War II, Jewish immigration to Palestine soared, as did Arab opposition. Just as the war began, the political situation for the Jews in the Holy Land deteriorated, so that immigration was virtually curtailed. This left millions of Jews, who might have migrated to the Promised Land, trapped in Hitler's Europe. Tragically, millions of them perished in the Holocaust.

After the end of World War II, the United States, under the leadership of President Harry Truman, convinced the British to allow one hundred thousand Jews living in European refugee camps to immigrate to Palestine. This opened a floodgate of Jewish immigration from all over the world back to their land.

On November 29, 1947, at Lake Success, New York, the United Nations, with a vote of 33 to 13, declared that the State of Israel, having been dormant for twenty-five hundred years, should be reborn.[26] This event fulfilled a number of biblical prophecies after the Babylonians led the Jews into captivity.

The words of the Old Testament prophet Isaiah come to mind:

> Who has heard such a thing?
> Who has seen such things?
> Shall the earth be made to give birth in one day?
> Or shall a nation be born at once?
> For as soon as Zion was in labor,
> She gave birth to her children.[27]
>
> He will set up a banner for the nations,
> And will assemble the outcasts of Israel,
> And gather together the dispersed of Judah
> From the four corners of the earth.[28]

With the founding of the nation of Israel, it was as if the world was watching before its very eyes what the prophet Ezekiel spoke about:

> The hand of the LORD came upon me and brought me out in the Spirit of the LORD, and set me down in the midst of the valley; and

> it was full of bones . . . Then He said to me, "Son of man, these bones are the whole house of Israel. They indeed say, 'Our bones are dry, our hope is lost, and we ourselves are cut off!' Therefore prophesy and say to them, 'Thus says the Lord GOD: "Behold, O My people, I will open your graves and cause you to come up from your graves, and bring you into the land of Israel."'"[29]

Jeremiah foretold:

> But I will gather the remnant of My flock out of all countries where I have driven them, and bring them back to their folds; and they shall be fruitful and increase.[30]

Micah asserted:

> I will surely assemble all of you, O Jacob, I will surely gather the remnant of Israel; I will put them together like sheep of the fold, like a flock in the midst of their pasture; they shall make a loud noise because of so many people.[31]

The Jews once more had reclaimed the land promised to them by God through Abraham.

The very next day, after the infant nation was reborn, Israel was attacked on all sides by armies representing Arab League countries. Their objective: to drive the Jews into the Mediterranean and reclaim the land for themselves. Israel defeated them.

In 1956, eight years later, the region once again exploded in all-out war. Again, the nation of Israel survived.

In 1967, in what was known as the "Six Day War," Israel defeated its Arab enemies by crushing the armies of Syria, Egypt, and Jordan. The nation of Israel was again victorious.

In 1973, in what was known as the Yom Kippur War, Egypt and Syria again attempted to destroy the State of Israel and, in a surprise attack, almost defeated them. Once again, Israel survived.

Blood flowed then, and it flows yet today.

Hundreds of thousands of Palestinian Arabs have been displaced and, tragically, they have ended up in refugee camps scattered throughout the Middle East. From these camps of misery and despair come many of the terrorists and suicide bombers today.

The question remains: Who does this land belong to? The land called Israel belongs first and foremost to God. God says clearly in His Word: "The land shall not be sold permanently, for the land is Mine."[32] Only God, whose land it is, has the right to bestow "land rights." There is no doubt that God gave it to Abraham, Isaac, and Jacob. Because of disobedience by Abraham and his descendants through the centuries, today the world is faced with this quagmire. The only One who has the answers to this dilemma, hatred, and bloodshed is the Lord Jesus Christ.

Although such news does not make headlines, there are Arabs and Jews that coexist harmoniously in Israel. Peace is possible.

Jesus loved His people and their land.

> O Jerusalem, Jerusalem, the one who kills the prophets and stones those who are sent to her! How often I wanted to gather your children together, as a hen gathers her chicks under her wings, but you were not willing! See! Your house is left to you desolate; for I say to you, you shall see Me no more till you say, "Blessed is He who comes in the name of the LORD!"[33]

The name *Jerusalem* means "the foundation of peace." There will be peace in Jerusalem one day. I pray that day will come soon—when the Prince of Peace, the King of kings, the Name above all names, returns. "Pray for the peace of Jerusalem: 'May they prosper who love you.'"[34]

THE ROOT PROBLEM

To sum all this up, what is the root of the problem in the Middle East today? In one word, it is sin.

Whose sin? Is it the Jews'?

Yes.

Is it the Arabs'?

Yes.

It is traced all the way back to the father of them both, Abraham, when he and Sarah grew impatient in waiting for God's blessing—the son of the promise—Isaac.

The turmoil that resulted from this sin has reached even to the shores of this country—a place called Ground Zero.

17

THE DEVIL'S DOORSTEP

I felt like I was standing on the front porch of hell.

The sight of total destruction, the smell of death, and a thin haze of dust and smoke clung to the air. Ground Zero in Lower Manhattan's Battery Park, on this day, seemed to be the Devil's doorstep.

New York City's famed Mayor Rudy Giuliani had invited me to give the closing prayer at a family memorial service to honor those who had died in the World Trade Center attacks on September 11.

A temporary platform stood near the mangled steel girders and rubble pit, known as "the pile," where just seven weeks earlier, two of the world's tallest towers imploded. After taking my seat on the makeshift platform next to the mayor and other dignitaries and participants, I reflected on the surreal scene.

Behind me, smoke—created by seeping gases and fires still not extinguished since the terrorist attacks—spewed from beneath pieces of concrete, rebar, glass, and other refuse. Hoses from fire trucks streamed water into the cauldron, the spray turning to steam that mingled with smoke from the fires. A fine, nearly imperceptible dust settled on my hair, skin, and clothing.

The most hideous invasion of my senses, though, was the stench from still-burning jet fuel and the incineration of hundreds of pulverized bodies.

An American flag hung from a pole in the center of the pile. On a nearby building, a sign read, "We Will Never Forget." That is why we were there: to help remember the dead. Not just firemen, policemen, and tower residents or visitors had perished in the collapse of the buildings. Pilots, flight attendants, passengers—all had fallen into this common grave. Every person who died that tragic day left behind families who now grappled with loss, grief, and unanswered questions.

I could not shake the thought: *This is a picture of hell—the bleak devastation, unquenchable fire, and stench of death.* The grim hopelessness made me shudder.

The recovery of human remains continued around the clock. Anytime a recognizable fragment of flesh was discovered, a horn sounded and all workers ceased activity. An ambulance was summoned, and the attendants brought a stretcher. The discovered body parts were carefully inserted into body bags with dignity. The workers then formed two lines and stood at respectful attention as the stretcher moved between them to the ambulance. Only after the vehicle had rolled out of sight on its way to the morgue would recovery and cleanup resume at Ground Zero.

These faithful crews worked twelve-hour shifts night and day, sifting carefully through thousands of tons of debris and dirt now contaminated by the body fluids of the dead.

But the sobering picture of death and destruction behind me was matched by a different panorama of sadness before me: Thousands of family members awaited the prayer service, most of them eyeing for the first time the crime scene where their loved ones tragically perished.

They sat quietly, some wearing white masks to reduce inhalation of pollution and odor, in long rows of folding chairs jammed into the streets and open spaces. Thousands were seated, but even more stood packed together, a sea of faces stretching for blocks.

The crowd included infant to gray-haired, famous and common, American and foreign, black and white—of every creed and faith. Shrouded in hollow expressions, many held photos in their laps, occasionally lifting the picture frame to the sky in memory of lost loves and broken dreams. Their strained faces revealed inner thoughts, silent pleas expressed in tears that cried out, "Why?"

Tiny urns, filled with earth dug from the scene, were presented to each family. For many, this would be the only closure because hundreds of the bodies would never be recovered. Cable news reported that one child said about the container, "Now I have my mommy." My heart broke over the human pain that the sins of angry, evil men had visited on the innocent.

Now on October 28, work had stopped for the first time at Ground Zero since September 11, and firemen and others laboring in the rubble stood, heads bare, hard hats clutched to their hearts.

The service began with an honor guard marching in the colors. The national anthem was sung by a New York police officer named Daniel Rodriguez. Music and prayers were interspersed. Since this was an interfaith service, representatives of Islam, Judaism, and Christianity participated, and Renee Fleming of the Metropolitan Opera sang "Amazing Grace."

As I watched and listened, I yearned to offer words of hope to these thousands of hurting families. They had lost mothers, fathers, husbands, wives, sons, daughters, brothers, sisters—dear friends, and no one could bring them back.

Before delivering the benediction, I said, "Today, I stand before you as a minister of the Christian faith."

And then I prayed:

Our Father, which art in heaven
Hallowed be Your Name,
And hallowed is the ground upon which we stand,
Your kingdom come, Your will be done, on earth as it is in heaven

We come to You this day to seek Your help, Your mercy, and Your grace.
We pray today that You will surround these families with Your love and that You will comfort them during this time of great personal loss . . .

God is our refuge and strength,
A very present help in trouble.[1]

But those who wait on the LORD
Shall renew their strength;
They shall mount up with wings like eagles,
They shall run and not be weary,
They shall walk and not faint.[2]

As we grieve today we are reminded of Your grief and the sacrifice You made for all mankind when You sent Your Son, Jesus Christ, to this earth to die for our sins on Calvary's cross and the hope that we have through the power of His Name. What hope is there outside of the Name of the Lord Jesus Christ?

For I am persuaded that neither death nor life, nor angels nor principalities nor powers, nor things present nor things to come, nor height nor depth, nor any other created thing, shall be able to separate us from the love of God which is in Christ Jesus our Lord.[3]

As I concluded my prayer and looked into the faces of the thousands in front of me, I wished I could do something more as the grief and pain were overwhelming.

Hell is going to be eternity filled with grief and pain, an unquenchable fire, according to the Bible. I could not help but think of the life that we have now and the breath that God has given us. On that September day, not one of the people who died could have imagined that their life would come to such an abrupt and tragic end that morning. It is important that all of us live our lives for Him in the knowledge of His truth and through faith in the Name of His Son; for we never know when our lives will end.

SEIZING HOPE

We have looked at the controversy surrounding this Name. It is obvious that no other single person in history has influenced human events more than Jesus Christ.

I want to ask you a pointed question: If you had been in the World Trade Towers that morning of 9/11, would you have been ready for death? Most of us do not dwell on the thought of death. A visit to Ground Zero causes one to give it some thought. Whether God blesses us with a long life or a short life, there is one thing we all have in common—the grave. Eventually, whether in a tragedy like the World Trade Center, from cancer in a hospital bed, or a heart attack in our sleep, we all will face death someday. Do you know your eternal destiny?

I have shared much about the Name above all names. But knowledge about God never saved anyone. It is not enough to know the story of Jesus. You must know Him personally.

The Bible makes it very clear that God loves us. He cares for us and He wants us to live our lives to the fullest. But for most people, there is emptiness in their lives that they can't explain. Something is missing. They search for it, through various religions, through relationships, through the acquisition of things money can buy, but that emptiness is still in the pit of their soul. There is a vacuum inside all of us—it can only be filled by God when we come into a right relationship to Him.

We can have a relationship with Him. How? Through His Son, Jesus Christ. He is the mediator between God and man. He is not still hanging on a Roman cross. He is alive in heaven—and He loves you. You can have a new life of meaning and purpose, free from guilt. How does that occur? I want to pose a few simple questions that will clarify the facts concerning the most important decision any person will ever make.

Do you feel that something is missing deep down in your very soul?

Do you feel an emptiness that you cannot explain—sometimes a loneliness—even though you may be in the midst of a crowd?

Most people do. In moments when we are most thoughtful about the meaning of life, there is a craving for something more. At its core, this is a longing to know God intimately. Often people try to fill this emptiness with other things—like alcohol, drugs, food, sexual adventures. The list is long. However, none of these can fill this emptiness, or take away this inner loneliness.

The truth is that God wants to supply what is missing deep inside your soul. He wants to have a relationship with all of us. Each one of us must make a choice to let God into our lives.

We need to understand what it takes to have a right relationship with God; for one day, we will all stand before Him.

What separates you from God? What causes that emptiness in your life?

It is sin.

In today's tolerant culture where "anything goes," many do not understand what sin means. Sin is breaking God's laws. When you disobey God's laws, it separates you from Him.

No matter how hard we try, none of us are able to live life without breaking God's laws. The Bible says: "For all have sinned and fall short of the glory of God,"[4] and "the wages of sin is death."[5] This is the price, this is the penalty . . . this is the sentence. The Supreme Judge—God Himself—has proclaimed that all of mankind is guilty. Everyone has a sin problem. There is no escaping this because God is morally perfect and "holy" and demands that anyone who comes near Him must be holy too.

So how do we as sinners ever solve this dilemma? God's answer comes through the perfect life, death, and resurrection of a substitute sacrifice for our sins—the Lamb of God, His Son—the Lord Jesus Christ. He is the One who paid our debt of sin. We could not possibly pay it.

The Bible tells us, "God so loved the world that He gave His only begotten Son, that whoever believes on Him should not perish but have everlasting life."[6]

And that "whoever" is you and me. Jesus is the only way to God, because He is the only One in history to take sin's penalty for you and me. Buddha did not die for our sins; Muhammad did not die for our sins. No one paid the debt of sin for us except the Lord Jesus Christ—when He shed His blood on Calvary's cross, went to the grave, and rose again on the third day. The only way we can come to God is by faith through His Son and Him alone.

Jesus is the only door we can pass through to meet God the Father.

Do you believe? Are you willing to trust Jesus Christ as your personal Savior? What is your response?

Do not put off making a decision for Christ. The Bible says, "Behold, now is . . . the day of salvation."[7]

"God . . . desires all men to be saved from their sins and to come to the knowledge of the truth. For there is one God and one Mediator between God and men, the Man Christ Jesus, who gave Himself a ransom for all."[8]

We must all put our faith in Jesus Christ. The Bible says that Christ came into the world to save sinners.[9] Salvation is free to anyone who calls on the Lord Jesus Christ and repents of their sin. It is a gift from God that one can accept. The Bible says," The gift of God is eternal life in Christ Jesus our Lord."[10]

A story was told years ago about a man who was imprisoned for murder. Because he was a model prisoner, the governor decided to offer him a pardon. When the warden came into his cell and told him that the governor had pardoned him and that he was free to go, he refused the pardon. They were bewildered. The case had to go back to the courts to see if the condemned had the right to refuse the governor's pardon. The courts had no choice but to carry out the execution of the condemned man. This is the way it is with us. Because of our sin, we are condemned and sentenced to death; but God offers us a pardon—through receiving His Son, Jesus Christ, by faith. The point is that you have to be willing to accept the pardon.

"How do I do that?" you may ask. "How can I trust this Name above all names, and experience a new and vibrant life, free from guilt and shame?"

It is simple.

First, you must be willing to confess your sins to God, ask Him for forgiveness, and tell Him that you want to change and turn from the sinful life you have been living.

Next, by faith, ask Jesus Christ to come into your life, take control of your life, and to be the Lord of your life.

Then, follow Him from this day forward by obeying Him and reading His instructions found in His Word, the Holy Bible.

If you are willing to do that, God will forgive you and cleanse you. He will give you a new life and a new beginning. As you close this book, you can have that assurance that you have been saved, and that one of these days, when death comes for you, you will have nothing to fear. You will know that for eternity you will be safe in the presence of the King of kings and Lord of lords.

If your desire is to accept Christ as your Savior now, just pray this prayer:

> Dear God, I am a sinner. I am sorry for my sins. Forgive me. I believe that Jesus Christ is Your Son. I believe that Jesus Christ died for my sins. I want to invite Him into my life. I want to trust Him as my Savior and follow Him as my Lord, from this day forward, forevermore. In Jesus' Name, amen.

If you have prayed that prayer and meant it, I want you to know that God has forgiven you and cleansed you. Your name is now recorded in the Lamb's Book of Life. This is the record of everyone in history who has trusted the Savior. Your name is written there, and it can never be erased.

THE NAME ABOVE ALL NAMES

The brilliant and intense Jewish man—in chains busily writing letter after letter in his Roman jail cell—understood the magnificence of the Name.

The Apostle Paul, in one affectionate note to some old friends in another city, wrote joyfully about why the Name of Jesus reigns above all others:

> And being found in appearance as a man, He humbled Himself and became obedient to the point of death, even the death of the cross. Therefore God also has highly exalted Him and given Him the name which is above every name, that at the name of Jesus every knee should bow, of those in heaven, and of those on earth, and of those under the earth, and that every tongue should confess that Jesus Christ is Lord, to the glory of God the Father.[11]

While our King and Lord waits for the moment when the Father will end human history and authorize Jesus to return—this time not as a humble baby but in the clouds where every eye will see Him[12]—Jesus sits in a place of honor at the right hand of God the Father. He is not idle! Jesus came as a servant, and He is still serving today by interceding on our behalf, at His Father's right hand, through prayer.

> But [Jesus], because He continues forever, has an unchangeable priesthood. Therefore He is also able to save to the uttermost those who come to God through Him, since He always lives to make intercession for them.[13]

Not only is He making intercession for us. He is also preparing us a place. Jesus said:

> Let not your heart be troubled; you believe in God, believe also in Me. In My Father's house are many mansions; if it were not so, I would have told you. I go to prepare a place for you. And if I go and prepare a place for you, I will come again and receive you to Myself; that where I am, there you may be also.[14]

Some day—could it be today?—the trumpet will sound. In Jesus' own words, here's what will happen:

> When the Son of Man comes in His glory, and all the holy angels with Him, then He will sit on the throne of His glory. All the nations will be gathered before Him . . .[15]

Our God is a gracious and patient Father, but when He lowers the curtain on mankind's story, the play will be over.

As Paul wrote in that letter to his friends at Philippi, every knee will bow and every tongue will confess, "Jesus Christ is Lord."

All knees will bow and every tongue will confess, including:

Abraham, the pharaohs, Moses, Mary and Joseph, the disciples
John the Baptist, the Pharisees, Herod, Pilate, the Apostle Paul
Roman emperors, Alexander the Great, Constantine
Winners and losers
Columbus, Cortés, Perry, Lindberg, Armstrong
Popes, Muhammad, Mahatma Gandhi, Mother Teresa
Washington, Lincoln, Roosevelt, Kennedy, Reagan
Kings, queens, princes, and princesses
George Wishart, Cassie Bernall, and all martyrs wearing their white robes
Babe Ruth, Tiger Woods, Joe Montana, America's Cup winners
Mark McGwire, Muhammad Ali
Abortionists and anti-abortionists
Stalin, Hitler, Lenin, Mao, Pol Pot, Bin Laden
Members of the nearly ten thousand religions
Construction workers and doctors
Frank Sinatra, Cher, Michael Jackson, Madonna
Marilyn Monroe, Jimmy Stewart, Mel Gibson, Julia Roberts
Martin Luther and Martin Luther King
Millionaires and misfits
Carnegie, Vanderbilt, Rockefeller, Walton, Gates
Moonshiners, mafia, drug lords, pushers, and addicts
Bunyan, Shakespeare, Hemingway, Lewis, Grisham
Pornographers, prostitutes, philanthropists, and pedophiles
Larry King, Barbara Walters, David Letterman, Tom Brokaw
Patriots and terrorists
Van Gogh, Michelangelo, Picasso, Rockwell
Saddam Hussein, Yasir Arafat
Golda Meir, David Ben Gurion, Ariel Sharon

Rachel the Israeli victim and Ayat the suicide bomber
Lawyers and longshoremen
Mozart, Beethoven, Gershwin, Lennon
Skeptics and mockers
Voltaire, Freud, Darwin, Madeline Murray O'Hare
Billy and Ruth Graham
Franklin Graham
Your boss and your neighbor
Your spouse and your child
You

Every knee will bow and every tongue will confess, "Jesus Christ is Lord."

Dear friends of our family, Bill and Gloria Gaither, years ago penned words that say it so well:

Jesus, Jesus, Jesus,
    There's just something about that Name
    Master, Savior, Jesus,
    like the fragrance after the rain . . .
    Jesus, Jesus, Jesus,
    let all heaven and earth proclaim
    kings and kingdoms will all pass away
    but there's something about that Name.
Jesus, the mere mention of His Name
    can calm the storm, heal the broken, and raise the dead . . .
At the Name of Jesus
    I've seen sin-hardened men melt, Derelicts transformed
    the lights of hope put back into the eyes of a hopeless child . . .
At the Name of Jesus
    hatred and bitterness turn to love and forgiveness
    arguments cease . . .
I've heard a mother softly breathe His Name
    at the bedside of a child delirious from fever
    and I've watched that little body grow quiet
    and the fevered brow cool . . .

I've sat beside a dying saint
her body racked with pain
who in those final fleeting seconds summoned her last ounce of
having strength
to whisper earth's sweetest Name, Jesus, Jesus . . .
Emperors have tried to destroy it
Philosophies have tried to stamp it out
Tyrants have tried to wash it from the face of the earth
with the very blood of those who claimed it
yet still it stands . . .
And there shall be that final day
when every voice that has ever uttered a sound
every voice of Adam's race
shall raise in one great mighty chorus
to proclaim the Name of Jesus . . .
For in that day every knee shall bow
and every tongue shall confess
that Jesus Christ is Lord.
So you see . . .
it wasn't by mere chance
that caused the angel one night long ago
to say to a virgin maiden
His Name shall be called
Jesus, Jesus, Jesus . . .
You know . . .
there is something about that Name.[16]

And then those from every generation, who have believed in the Name and accepted the gift of eternal life, will together worship the King:

And they sang a new song . . .

"For You were slain, . . .
And have redeemed us to God by Your blood

> Out of every tribe and tongue and people and nation . . .
> And we shall reign on the earth."

And every creature which is in heaven and on the earth and under the earth and such as are in the sea, and all that are in them, I heard saying:

> "Blessing and honor and glory and power
> Be to Him who sits on the throne,
> And to the Lamb, forever and ever!"[17]

One day we will all stand before Jesus, either as our Savior or our Judge. I don't know about you, but I am ready to face the One who is owed all the glory and honor, the One who bears the Name—**JESUS.**

NOTES

CHAPTER I

1. Internet, www.salon.com, 27 January 2001. Accessed 28 April 2002.
2. Internet, www.humanismbyjoe.com. Accessed 28 April 2002.
3. Marvin Olasky, "The Greatest Spin Ever Sold," *World*, May/June 2002, 9.
4. S. Dhammika, "Famous People Comment on the Buddha and His Teachings," http://web.singnet.com.sg/~sidneys/praises5.htm. Accessed 4 May 2002.
5. John 1:46 NKJV.
6. John 7:7 NKJV.
7. Michael F. McCauley, compiler and editor, *The Jesus Book* (Chicago: The Thomas More Press, 1978), 41.
8. Quoted in D. James Kennedy and Jerry Newcombe, *What If Jesus Had Never Been Born?* (Nashville: Thomas Nelson Publishers, 1994), 5.
9. McCauley, *The Jesus Book*, 188.
10. Quoted in Kennedy and Newcombe, *What If Jesus Had Never Been Born?*, 6.
11. Les Sellars, "Western Intellectual Leaders Discuss Christianity," *World* Magazine, May/June 2002, 51.
12. 1 Peter 4:14, 16 NIV.
13. Internet, www.ccci.org, "Who Is Jesus?" Accessed on 28 April 2002.
14. Josh McDowell, *Evidence that Demands a Verdict*, Volume 1 (Nashville: Thomas Nelson Publishers, 1979), 106.

15. Calvin Miller, *The Book of Jesus* (New York: Simon & Schuster, 1996), 290.
16. Colossians 1:15–20 NIV.
17. Acts 2:21 NKJV.
18. John 1:12 NKJV.

CHAPTER 2

1. John 11:25–26 NKJV.
2. Virginia Culver, "Tone of Service Angers Some," *Denver Post*, 29 April 1999, A8.

CHAPTER 3

1. George W. Bush, *A Charge to Keep* (New York: William Morrow, 1999), 136.
2. Matthew 10:32 NKJV.
3. Alan M. Dershowitz, "Bush Starts Off by Defying the Constitution," *Los Angeles Times*, 24 January 2001, B.9.
4. Cathy Lynn Grossman, "Some Call Inaugural Prayers to Jesus Exclusionary," *USA Today*, 24 January 2001, 10D.
5. Patrick Henry, American Foundation Publications, "Famous Quotes." Accessed via the Internet 25 February 2002.
6. Jeff Jacoby, "Jesus Should Not Be a Forbidden Word in America," *Atlanta Journal-Constitution*, 4 February 2001, C11.
7. Ibid.
8. "No Offense in Christian Invocation," Letter to the Editor, *The Jewish Press*, 9 February 2001, 4.
9. Ben Fisher, "Illusion of Religious Unity Divides," *Daily Kent Stater*, 26 January 2001.
10. Ravi Zacharias, *Jesus Among Other Gods* (Nashville: Word Publishing, 2000), 158.
11. John 14:6 NKJV.

CHAPTER 4

1. See Daniel 4:25.
2. 2 Corinthians 1:3 NKJV.
3. 2 Thessalonians 2:7 NKJV.
4. Matthew 12:35 NKJV.
5. National Day of Prayer and Remembrance, Washington, D.C., Interview during *CNN Live*, 14 September 2001.
6. 1 John 3:8 NKJV.

7. E-mail from Tom Mangham to his parents, T. Grady and Evelyn Mangham, 16 September 2001.

CHAPTER 5

1. EP News Service, 17 January 2002, Bryon, California, pg. 11.
2. http://www.josh.org/project911/tolerance.asp
3. Ravi Zacharias, *Jesus Among Other Gods* (Nashville: Word Publishing, 2000), vii, 4.
4. Focus on the Family, *Citizen*, Web site, "The Wall That Never Was."
5. http://www.pbs.org/jefferson/enlight/prayer.htm
6. Boys of Sudan-American Red Cross, 14 August 2001, redcross.org. Accessed 14 April 2002.
7. J. Christy Wilson, Jr., *More to Be Desired Than Gold* (South Hamilton, Mass.: Gordon-Conwell Theological Seminary, 1998), 172–73; 121–22.
8. Luke 6:22–23 NKJV.
9. Matthew 10:5–8, 16–18 NKJV.
10. Acts 4:12 NKJV.
11. John 15:18–21 NKJV.
12. John 4:5–26 NKJV.
13. See Matthew 13:24–30.
14. Matthew 5:38–39, 43–45 NKJV.
15. See Exodus 20:3.
16. See Hebrews 11:9–10.

CHAPTER 6

1. Toby Lester, "Oh, Gods!" *The Atlantic Monthly*, February 2002, 38.
2. C. S. Lewis, *Mere Christianity* (New York: Macmillan Publishing Co., Inc., 1952), 56.
3. "For the Record," *National Review*, 5 November 2001, 6.
4. Exodus 20:3 NKJV.
5. Psalm 135:15–18 NKJV.
6. Hebrews 1:1–3 NIV.
7. 1 Kings 16:30 NKJV.
8. 1 Kings 18:18 NKJV.
9. 1 Kings 18:21–39 NIV.
10. Isaiah 43:10–11 NKJV.
11. Matthew 7:13–14 NKJV.
12. Ibn Taymiyyah, al-Jihad, edited by Dr. Abd al-Rahman Umayra, second edition, Beirut : Dar al-Jil, 1997, p. 48.

13. Koran Sura 2:256.
14. William F. Buckley Jr., "So You Want a Holy War?" *National Review*, 5 November 2001, 71.
15. Al Jaami- Al Saheeh by Imam Al Bukhari, Oral Collections known as the Hadith, Section 4:506.
16. Roy W. Gustafson.
17. Sura 2:116; 5:72–76; 6:101; 9:30; 10:68–69; 35:91.
18. Sura 9:5.
19. Judith Miller, "Mideast Turmoil: Arab Opinion; In Interview, Arafat's Wife Praises Suicide Bombings," *New York Times*, 14 April 2002.
20. Ravi Zacharias, *Jesus Among Other Gods* (Nashville: Word Publishing, 2000), 158–59.
21. Roy W. Gustafson.
22. See Ephesians 5:28–29.
23. Hadith (SD), 10 May 2002.
24. See Mark 5:25–34.
25. See John 8:3–11.
26. See Mark 16:7.
27. R.C. Sproul, "A Rose Is a Rose," *Tabletalk*, April 1998, 8.
28. Sura 2:25; 3:15; 3:198; 4:57; 37:41–49; 38:50–52, 52:17–20; 55:46–78.
29. The book of the Revelation.
30. John 14:6 NKJV.
31. Dean C. Halverson, gen. editor, *The Compact Guide to World Religion*, (Minneapolis: Bethany House, Pub. 1996), 90.
32. Ephesians 2:8–9 NKJV.
33. John 14:6 NKJV.
34. Preston G. Parrish quote.
35. Roy W. Gustafson quote.

CHAPTER 7

1. Proverbs 22:1 NIV.
2. Ecclesiastes 7:1 NIV.
3. See Genesis 2:19.
4. See Genesis 3:20..
5. *Bible Almanac*, 445.
6. Genesis 17:5 NKJV.
7. Hebrews 11:24–26 NKJV.
8. Exodus 3:1–14 NKJV.

9. *Nelson's Illustrated Bible Dictionary* (Nashville: Thomas Nelson Publishers, 1986), 427.
10. Ibid., 428.
11. John 10:14 NKJV.
12. Roy Gustafson, "In His Land Seeing Is Believing," *World Wide Publications*, 1980.
13. Henry Holley.
14. David Gonzales, "U.S. Aids Conversion-Minded Quake Relief in El Salvador," *New York Times,* 5 March 201, A3. Headlines noted appeared March 6–8, 2001, in local newspapers in Elizabeth City, N.C., DuQuoin, Ill., and Kannapolis, N.C.
15. "USAID Funding of Samaritan's Purse," U.S. Agency for International Development Statement, Washington, D.C., 7 March 2001.
16. Matthew 5:37 NKJV.

CHAPTER 8

1. C. S. Lewis, The Cumberland River Lamp Post—An Appreciation for C.S. Lewis; http://www.crlamppost.org/footprnt.thm, Accessed 28 April 2002.
2. John 1:1–3 NKJV.
3. See Genesis 15:5.
4. Genesis 22:1–14 NKJV.
5. *New Bible Dictionary*, "Roman Empire," 921, and "Judea," 605.
6. Micah 5:2 NIV.
7. *The Bible Almanac*, 1114.
8. *New Bible Dictionary*, "Roman Empire," 921–22.
9. *Thompson Chain Reference Bible*, 1699.
10. *The Bible Almanac*, 644, 711; *New Bible Dictionary*, 557.
11. Matthew 1:20–21 NKJV.
12. Luke 1:41 NKJV.
13. See Luke 1:76.
14. John 3:30 NKJV.
15. Matthew 11:5 NKJV.
16. Matthew 11:11 NKJV.
17. Matthew 14:1–12 NKJV.

CHAPTER 9

1. John 2:1–4 NKJV.
2. J. Vernon McGee, *Thru the Bible*, Vol. IV, 378.

3. "Palestine," *New Bible Dictionary* (Nashville: Thomas Nelson Publishers, 1986), 790.
4. John 15:20–21 NKJV.
5. John 16:23 NKJV.
6. See Acts 1:8.
7. See Acts 22:20.
8. Acts 9:4–6 NKJV.
9. Acts 9:15–16 NKJV.
10. 2 Corinthians 11:23–28 NKJV.
11. "Paul, The Apostle," *New Bible Dictionary* (Nashville: Thomas Nelson Publishers, 1986), 808.
12. John Foxe, *Christian Martyrs of the World* (Uhrichsville, Ohio: Barbour and Company, 1989), 82.
13. Acts 21:13 NKJV.
14. Revelation 6:9–11 NKJV.
15. Revelation 20:4 NKJV.
16. Matthew 10:39 NKJV.
17. Jim Elliott quotes.
18. Eugene Myers Harrison, "The Cobbler Who Turned Discoverer," *Giants of the Missionary Trail*, www.wholesomewords.org. Accessed on 12 February 2002.
19. Ibid.
20. Eugene Myers Harrison, "The Pathfinder of Africa," *Giants of the Missionary Trail*, www.wholesomewords.org. Accessed on 12 February 2002.
21. Ibid.

CHAPTER 10

1. William I. Koch, "Teamwork, Technology and Talent: The T3 Approach," accessed at www.a3.org, 12 February 2002.
2. Some details Paul C. Larsen, *To the Third Power: The Inside Story of Bill Koch's Winning Strategies for The America's Cup* (Gardiner, Maine: Tilbury House Publishers, 1995), 216–18.
3. Philippians 3:12–14 NKJV.
4. Matthew 28:19–20 NKJV.
5. 2 Chronicles 6:7 NKJV.
6. 2 Chronicles 6:8 NKJV.
7. "Hernán Cortés," *The World Book Encyclopedia*, Vol. 4 (Chicago: World Book, Inc.), 1074.
8. John Foxe, *Foxes Christian Martyrs of the World* (Uhrichsville, Ohio: Barbour and Company, 1989), 5–9.

9. Matthew 11:12 NIV.
10. John 15:13 NIV.
11. John 13:35 NIV.

CHAPTER 11

1. Luke 4:17–21 NKJV.
2. John 8:34–36 NKJV.
3. Romans 4:7–8 NIV
4. See Acts 26:18.

CHAPTER 12

1. Mark 10:37 NKJV.
2. Mark 10:43–45 NKJV.
3. See John 19:27.
4. See John 5:2–8.
5. See Luke 8:43–48.
6. See Luke 7:2–10.
7. Matthew 19:14 NKJV.
8. See Matthew 14:14–21.
9. See Matthew 15:32–38.
10. See Matthew 19:16–24.
11. Mark 8:36 NKJV.
12. Luke 7:13–15 NKJV.
13. See Matthew 15:22–28.
14. Matthew 11:28 NKJV.
15. See Luke 8:27–39 NKJV.
16. Luke 23:43.

CHAPTER 13

1. Deuteronomy 10:17–19 NKJV.
2. Luke 9:23 NKJV.

CHAPTER 14

1. Acts 4:7–10 NKJV.
2. Acts 3:6 NKJV.
3. John Pollock, A *Foreign Devil in China* (Minneapolis: World Wide Publications, 1988), 94.

4. Luke 4:38–39 NKJV.
5. Matthew 15:31 NKJV.
6. Matthew 4:23–25 NKJV.
7. Luke 18:35–43 NKJV.
8. John 5:2–9 NKJV.
9. Luke 5:12–13 NKJV.
10. Story originally appeared in "On Call," Publication of World Medical Mission, Fall 2001.
11. Story originally appeared in "On Call," Publication of World Medical Mission, Winter 2002.
12. Adapted from Lorry Lutz, *Sword & Scalpel/Robert L. Foster, M.D.* (Orange, Calif.: Promise Publishing, Inc., 1990), 93–96.

CHAPTER 15

1. Matthew 4:23–24 NKJV.
2. Mark 2:17 NKJV.
3. John 8:2–11 NKJV.
4. "AIDS Epidemic Update—December 2001, Global Overview," Joint United Nations Programme on HIV/AIDS, 1. Accessed on the Internet at www.unaids.org, June 6, 2002.
5. John 3:17 NKJV.
6. Amy Fagan, "Christians Urged to Act Against HIV," *Washington Times*, 19 February 2002.
7. Raju Chebium, "N.C. Doctor Finds His Faith Helps on AIDS Mission," Gannett News Service, 21 February 2002.
8. Uwe Siemon-Netto, "Evangelicals to Ponder AIDS Pandemic," UPI, 9 November 2001.
9. Sheler, "Prescription for Hope."
10. Sharon Begley, "AIDS at 20," *Newsweek*, 11 June 2001, 36.
11. Murphy, "'Army' of Christians," B4.
12. Siemon-Netto, "Evangelicals to Ponder."
13. Uwe Siemon-Netto, "Slow Church Response to AIDS Scolded," UPI, 18 February 2002.
14. Johanna McGeary, "Death Stalks a Continent," *Time* magazine, 12 February 2001. Acessed on the Internet at www.Time.com on 5 June 2002.
15. 1 Corinthians 7:2 NIV.
16. Caryle Murphy, "'Army' of Christians Needed in AIDS Fight, Evangelist Says," *Washington Post*, 19 February 2002, B1.

17. 1 Corinthians 13:4, 7–8 NKJV.
18. Matthew 25:40 NKJV.

CHAPTER 16

1. Jeremiah 6:14 NKJV.
2. Joshua Hammer, "How Two Lives Met in Death," *Newsweek*, 15 April 2002, 18.
3. Ezekiel 5:5 NKJV.
4. Isaiah 45:21–22 NKJV.
5. Zechariah 12:2–3 NKJV.
6. See Isaiah 2:1–5.
7. Roy Gustafson, "In His Land Seeing Is Believing," World Wide Publications, 1980.
8. Genesis 12:1–7 NKJV.
9. Genesis 21:18 NKJV.
10. *Nelson's Illustrated Bible Dictionary* (Nashville: Thomas Nelson, 1986), 518.
11. Exodus 6:8 NKJV.
12. Deuteronomy 31:16, 20 NKJV.
13. Judges 2:1–3 NKJV.
14. See 1 Samuel 8:6.
15. Psalm 44:11 NKJV.
16. Psalm 137:1 NIV.
17. Ezekiel 36:16–20 NKJV.
18. Luke 19:41–44 NKJV.
19. Norman Kotker, *The Earthly Jerusalem* (New York: Charles Scribner's Sons, 1969), 114.
20. Kotker, *The Earthly Jerusalem*, 115.
21. William Whiston, Trans., *The Works of Josephus*, "The Wars of the Jews," Book 5, 12:3 (Peabody, Mass.: Hendrickson Publishers, 1987), 723.
22. Whiston, *The Works of Josephus*, "The Wars of the Jews," Book 6, 4:6, 740.
23. Kotker, *The Earthly Jerusalem*, 117.
24. "Jerusalem," *World Book Encyclopedia*, Volume 11 (Chicago: World Book, Inc., 1988), 99.
25. "Palestine," *Encyclopedia Britannica*, 307.
26. Roy Gustafson, "In His Land Seeing Is Believing," World Wide Publications, 1980.
27. Isaiah 66:8 NKJV.
28. Isaiah 11:12 NKJV.

29. Ezekiel 37:1, 11–12 NKJV.
30. Jeremiah 23:3 NKJV.
31. Micah 2:12 NKJV.
32. Leviticus 25:23 NKJV.
33. Matthew 23:37–39 NKJV.
34. Psalm 122:6 NKJV.

CHAPTER 17

1. Psalm 46:1 NKJV.
2. Isaiah 40:31 NKJV.
3. Romans 8:38–39 NKJV.
4. Romans 3:23 NKJV.
5. Romans 6:23 NKJV.
6. John 3:16 NKJV.
7. 2 Corinthians 6:2 NKJV.
8. 1 Timothy 2:3–6 NKJV.
9. See 1 Timothy 1:15.
10. Romans 6:23 NKJV.
11. Philippians 2:8–11 NKJV.
12. See Revelation 1:7.
13. Hebrews 7:24–25 NKJV.
14. John 14:1–3 NKJV.
15. Matthew 25:31–32 NKJV.
16. "Jesus: There's Just Something About That Name," words by Bill and Gloria Gaither. Used by permission.
17. Revelation 5:9–10, 13 NKJV.

ACKNOWLEDGMENTS

I want to thank my wife, Jane Austin, who put up with a lot of my distractions while working on this project. She went through the manuscript carefully, giving me some very important input.

Special thanks to Bruce Nygren and Preston Parrish for their invaluable contribution. I couldn't have done it without them.

I am particularly grateful for the editorial input and advice from Charlotte DeMoss and Deborah Fonseca, who tirelessly spent hours reviewing each page and researching and verifying resource materials.

Others, such as Dr. Ross Rhoads, Rev. Skip Heitzig, Rev. Greg Laurie, Elizabeth DeMoss, Dr. Richard Furman, Dr. Melvin Cheatham, and Mark DeMoss were a great help to me in reviewing various aspects of the book. I certainly don't want to forget my dear friends in Lebanon who checked, and double-checked, the facts concerning the Middle East.

I want to express my personal thanks to Liz Toney and Paula Woodring for their help as we headed down the homestretch.

And of course, the one who has been the "glue," my secretary Donna Lee Toney.

ABOUT THE AUTHOR

FRANKLIN GRAHAM is chairman and president of Samaritan's Purse, a Christian relief and evangelistic organization. He is also president and CEO of the Billy Graham Evangelistic Association. Franklin is the fourth of Billy and Ruth Bell Graham's five children. He is the author of the bestselling autobiography *Rebel with a Cause, Living Beyond the Limits,* and the children's book *Miracle in a Shoebox.* An avid outdoorsman and pilot, Franklin and his wife, Jane Austin, have four children, two daughters-in-law, and one granddaughter, and they make their home in North Carolina.

In his autobiography, Franklin Graham tells his story of how God has taken his life and turned it into His Glory. Elizabeth Dole says, "Franklin has provided a very thoughtful and provocative account of how a young man develops and matures in his faith as the son of one of the world's most respected and admired spiritual leaders."

Rebel with a Cause

ISBN 0-7852-7170-8

AVAILABLE FALL 2002

The familiar phrase "it's who you know" is true for everyone; knowing the right people can make a difference in obtaining privileges, services, or assistance in daily life. By claiming the forgiveness of God purchased through the sinless life, death, and resurrection of the Lord Jesus Christ, everyone can be on a first-name basis and have a personal relationship with the most important person who has ever existed.

It's Who You know

ISBN 0-7852-6492-2